"Not long after I started
ed a revival meeting that c
evangelist was Dr. Glenn N
take a seemingly simple ve

Dr. Mathews' style of preaching has so affected my ministry that
it challenged me to further my education. I knew after hearing
him proclaim the Word of God that I wanted to be an expository preacher. Certainly, this book will be a blessing and will
challenge readers to know God and His Word better."

Dr. Gary Drake
Pastor, Clay First Baptist Church, Clay, WV
Board Member, Revival Crusade, inc.

"*Expositions That Encourage* is the appropriate title for a
book of twelve sermons that were preached and now published
by Dr. Glenn Mathews. I have heard him preach for over fifty
years and his messages are always expositions (explanation) of
the Word of God. I look forward to 'chewing the cud' of these
messages in printed form."

Dr. Bill Bartlett
President of the Board of Directors of Revival Crusade inc.

"I am honored to write a recommendation for this book written to encourage others. Glenn Mathews has certainly been an
encouragement to me for the 26 years during which time I have
served as Treasurer for Revival Crusade. I am also glad I can
use the talent God has given me in the area of accounting and
administration to encourage and support him."

Don Austin,
Treasurer, Revival Crusade inc.

"REVIVAL CRUSADE, iNC is one of the best Christian programs on the radio to hear the Gospel. Glenn also supports
many missionaries around the world and drives thousands of
miles to preach for different pastors and hold revivals and always preaches the Gospel. "

Jim Marrs,
Board member, Revival Crusade inc.

Several years ago as Glenn and I were returning from one of my eleven trips with him to Israel, I expressed to him, as others did, that he should write a book or books of some of his messages he has preached over the years. The first-hand knowledge he has gained by visiting and learning about people, their customs and conditions is amazing. It would be a wonderful training tool to those people who could read it and use it as they witness to people in all parts of the world. His unique blend of hard work, humor, authenticity and daily trusting the Lord, give him knowledge and strength to win many souls by his daily messages to those who will listen and change their life forever. To God be the glory!

Jack Gregory
Board Member, Revival Crusade, inc.

Expositions
that
Encourage

Scriptural thoughts to encourage your heart
by
Dr. Glenn Mathews

Truth Publishing
PO Box 104
Bennett, NC 27208

CreateSpace Independent Publishing Platform
© 2018 Truth Publishing
ISBN-13: 978-1984137746
ISBN-10: 1984137743

Cover Design: Tracy Jackson
Interior Design: Tracy Jackson
Editing: Tracy Glockle

This book is dedicated
to *Fleta, my treasure*

Acknowledgments

Where do I begin? If I were to acknowledge everyone who has influenced my life, the list would be longer than the book!

Surely, I must begin with Fleta, my life partner since 7/26/1958. Not until we are with the Lord will it be known the length, depth and height of her importance in our ministry. She has always been the greater prayer warrior, the stabilizing force (think anchor) and simultaneously the visionary of what God had in mind for our life's work . At the judgment seat I will need a very tall ladder on which to stand to see her, for she will be very far ahead of me in the receiving of rewards.

I must thank God for my parents, Rev. Ralph and Flora Mathews, who brought me up "in the fear and admonition of the Lord". Of course, countless preachers and teachers have had a positive impact upon me. Almost all of them have already finished their course and are off the scene. They, being dead, yet speak.

As for this book, I am indebted to many people. For the transcribers, Brenda Mattiazzo and Sherri Ward, I am grateful. To editors, Tracy Glockle and Tracy Jackson, I express my appreciation. To the members of the Board of Directors of Revival Crusade, Inc., I express my thanks for their support for over 41 years. They are among those who continually encouraged me in this endeavor. The one who "pushed and prodded" the most, was Dr. Neal Jackson. He has guided me through this entire ordeal (think opportunity)! As already stated, Fleta's input and patience, as the quintessential" help meet" was, is and will continue to be invaluable. This list is not exhaustive. Indeed, I am "debtor to all".

NOTE: I make one request of the reader. These sermons were preached in local church services. I, (we) have attempted to do as little editing as possible, so we can reflect the feeling of "being there". My request, then, is that you not just read, but "hear" the preaching. AMEN!

Table of Contents

Foreward

"The first time I heard Dr. Glenn Mathews preach, I sat in awe of the masterful way in which the sermon was presented. Since that first sermon, over 40 years ago, I have heard him preach hundreds of times. I have had him as an Evangelist in every church I have pastored. We have preached together on several mission fields, and have stood shoulder to shoulder on a number of trips to the Holy Land. I tell folks everywhere that he is my favorite preacher, and that I believe him to be the best living expositor of God's Word today!

For many years, I have encouraged him to take the time to put his sermons in a book. He has finally done that, and I am so glad to introduce these sermons to you. These messages need to be preserved for the generations to come. Should the Lord tarry His coming, the next generation will need these wonderful, fresh, Bible sermons. In my library, I have books of sermons from some of the great preachers of yesteryear-Spurgeon, Morgan, Rice, McCartney, and many others. Our generation has been blessed by the sermons of these great men of God.

Now, we can be encouraged and blessed by the preaching of a man who has been greatly used of God for many years in our generation. The expository style of preaching in these sermons will bless the heart of any person who reads them. They will inspire, explain, enlighten, and encourage. I hope you take the time to read each page and think about the hours of prayer, study, thought, and effort that went into each message, and allow the power of the Word of God to reach your heart.

Dr. Mathews has been my mentor, my Apostle Paul, my advisor, my teacher, but most of all, he has been my friend. His wisdom, Bible knowledge, discernment, and ability to take words and paint a picture will thrill your soul as you read these messages. I have had the benefit of those qualities throughout my entire ministry, for every time I have picked up the phone and called for help or advice, he has been there to help. That wisdom and discernment is now available for you as you read these sermons. I know you will enjoy each message!"

Dr. Norris E. Belcher, Jr.
Senior Pastor, Church of the Open Door, Westminster, MD
Vice President of the Board, Revival Crusade, inc.

Introduction

Though the years, I have been encouraged to "get something into print, write a book, and write a series of books" etc. More recently, it is "why have you not put your stuff into print?" If I am asked to speak extemporaneously, I am ready. But "to write" is an entirely different matter. Spoken words are soon forgotten. Written words remain. Spoken words may contain grammatical errors, and be overlooked. Writing, however, (in my mind) must be precise, perfect prose. So, I have yet to "write" a book.

The book you are holding is not the result of writing, but of compiling. I study, pray, prepare and preach messages. Others transcribe them. Still others edit them. I gave a nod of approval, and now a different group of others have published them.

Why this book? It is a response to the more than a few requests of people who, evidently, feel something that I have preached should be preserved in print. I express my sincere gratitude to those who urged me, guided and supported me in getting these sermons into print. It is up to the readers to determine their value.

My first sermon was preached on February 28, 1953, when I was a 17 year old high school senior. The sermon was an evangelistic one, preached at a youth rally in Cherry Street Baptist Church in Attalla, AL. I preached from Luke 16 on "Hell", (that was the full title) and spoke for only 11 minutes, even though I went through my notes twice! The length of my sermons has surely changed. I hope that the reader will note a change in the depth of these messages. I am convinced that every sermon that I have preached could have been delivered better with more effectiveness had I spent more time in preparation and prayer. These twelve efforts are surely in that category.

Why this particular book? Even before Fleta and I were married in 1958, we were involved in ministry, pastoring, teaching and counseling. For the last 41+ years we have given ourselves full-time to evangelism and missions. We have been privileged to serve on every continent except Antarctica (thank God for that exception). I always thought that my first book of sermons (if ever got it written) would be evangelistic in nature. I even imagined that a second book would be on homiletics (the art of the preparation and delivery of a sermon) designed as a textbook for use in classrooms for "preacher boys." When my imagination really got started, I could envision more than two or three books...e.g. *Twelve Terrific Talks on Abraham, The Gospel in all 50 chapters of Genesis, 100+ sermons from Ephesians* ... or even some books on Israel in Prophecy (as though no one else had done that) – Naive? Yes indeed.

On the surface, it appears a bit strange that an evangelist's first attempt at publishing should be on the subject of encouragement. Is that not one of the roles of the pastor? Yes, but – who is there that does not need and desire to be encouraged? With the rapid pace of change in the culture of our country (God bless the USA), with the increasing animosity toward Biblical Christianity and thus toward Christians, with the probable persecution that is looming, believers need to be encouraged in the faith that was once and for all delivered to the saints.

It is my prayer that these sermons will assist the reader to do as David did when he "encouraged himself in the Lord his God" I Samuel 30:6

First and last, this book is written to give glory to the Lord!

Chapter One

Serving in the Night
Psalm 134

Serving in the Night

Behold, bless ye the LORD, all ye servants of the LORD,
which by night stand in the house of the LORD.
Lift up your hands in the sanctuary, and bless the LORD.
The LORD that made heaven and earth bless thee out of Zion.
— Psalm 134:1

Psalm 134 is characterized as a song of degrees, or a song of steps. There are fifteen such songs, and this is the final one. They start in Psalm 120, and each of them builds until Psalm 134. There are evidences that these were songs that were sung on high holy days: Passover, Pentecost, and Tabernacles. And there also writings that indicate that these Psalms were sung as the people approached the temple on the south side of the temple mount.

At the south side of the temple mount, as you approach the wall, the gates are now closed and sealed over with blocks. But for these worshipers coming up to worship from the city of David, Gihon Springs, there are fifteen steps. There are wide steps, and then there is a little step that's about half that, and then another step wide and deep—fifteen such. And it's not a coincidence that there are fifteen. It's presumed that the people sang these songs, one at each of the steps as they came to the gates. They sang Psalm 133 as they entered the gates, and then 134, when they were on the temple mount.

The Psalm begins with "Behold." In fact, Psalm 133 begins that way, too. If you go back from Psalm 120 and read forward, there are about five psalms where the word "behold" is in the psalms, but only in Psalms 133 and 134 does the psalm begin with the word "behold." Let me define the word "behold" for you. It means amazement, to look at wide-eyed, slack-jawed, with an open mouth, to catch your breath. Any time you read the word "behold," that's what you'll think of. This Psalm begins this way.

You may think it's kind of anticlimactic, that the big Psalm is 133: brethren dwelling in unity, and the anointing of the Spirit. But the height of these songs of degrees is this one. In verse 1, "bless ye the LORD;" in verse 2, "bless the LORD;" in verse 3, "The LORD that made heaven and earth bless thee."

There are two divisions. Verses 1 and 2 speaks of our responsibility, while verse 3 speaks of God's response.

Bless the Lord in the Night

Behold, bless ye the LORD, all ye servants of the LORD, which by night stand in the house of the LORD. — Psalm 134:1

During the daytime on the temple mount, it's busy. There's activity everywhere, and there are a lot of people—sacrifices taking place, the choir singing, and parents coming to dedicate their 40-day-old babies to the Lord.

Rabbinical sources tell us that there were 600 people who were "employed" or working at the temple during the day. There was activity everywhere. But at night, these are all gone. There's this little skeleton crew at night. One source says that there was one temple guard, two priests, and 22 other Levites that worked at night. The Levite tribe is the tribe that had responsibility for caring for the temple. With the exception of these workers, nobody else was there. But these workers labored through the night, preparing for temple worship the next day. At night, it's almost deserted. It's quiet and dark. There are no big lights. The only light you have is a candle or lantern that you carry.

It's much easier to serve God in the light of day. You can have great fellowship with fellow believers in the day. But what do you do at night when it is dark and lonely? The natural tendency is to try to escape from the darkness. Just stay there. That's where God put you. There's much to be said for faithfulness. Stay put.

Just bloom where you're planted. I detest and admire dandelions. My next door neighbor, I think, has a dandelion farm, and all of that blows over into my yard. I've spent a lot of time and money trying to get rid of dandelions. I detest those things. You come through with the lawn mower cut it down to two inches. You can't even see it, but two days later, there it comes up again. It just keeps coming. Dandelions are a weed. They're a nuisance. I despise them, but I have to admire their stick-to-it-iveness. If only we had people like that.

Twenty-five years ago, I was most impressed by a young preacher who was doing a good job at a church in another state. One day, I got a call from some people who asked, "Can you recommend somebody to be our pastor?" I immediately thought of this man. This church was twice the size of the church he was in and would have paid him twice the money, if not more. But to my surprise, he said, "No, I'm not interested." When I asked him why, he said, "This is where God put me, and I think until God moves me, I'll just stay where I am." I recommended him a couple years later to another church, and the same thing happened. Three or four years later I recommended him to a third church, same thing. And do you know, he's still there. His church is not the biggest church in the county, and you'll never hear about him. But heaven knows him very well; he's faithful.

Do you know that the stars shine 24 hours a day? If you go down in a well and look up through the darkness, you can see the stars at noon. We don't see them in the day, only at night, in the darkness. You're going to see things and learn things in the dark that you'll never see and learn in the sunshine. So, bless the Lord, stand, stay where you are.

Worship the Lord in the Night

Lift up your hands in the sanctuary, and bless the LORD.
— Psalm 134:2

Wait a minute. It's dark, and I'm supposed to lift up my hands? Why? Don't think you are the only one in the dark. There are other people there, and they might be thinking, "I don't like working in the night." If you will lift up your hands, somebody near you is going to see that. You're not deserted. You're not by yourself. You're going to be an encouragement to somebody else.

When I was a child, my father the preacher went to visit an old lady in our congregation. She was born negative to the core. My daddy came back in after having seen her, and my mother said, "Well, how is she today?" My dad said, "She's complaining of feeling better." There are a lot of people like that. I know when I was pastoring, I would go to see certain people and be drained when I left. I would go to see other people who were equally as ill or just as much shut in as another, and I would leave blessed, rejoicing in the Lord, because the one that I went to see blessed me.

You don't know who you can encourage. You don't know who you can help. You're lifting up your hands and encouraging other people even though you're in the dark.

God's Response in the Night

The LORD that made heaven and earth bless thee out of Zion. — Psalm 134:3

Verses 1 and 2 are our responsibility. Verse 3 is God's response, and it says the Lord will bless you. He's the Lord that made heaven and earth. He's the Creator and the controller. I'd like to go to the Hubble telescope. I'm fascinated by what we're able to see in living color, worlds, planets, and solar systems that defy the mind. Just the beauty of it and the immensity of it, and to know that the God that I know, Jehovah God, made that and controls that. That's phenomenal.

In 1969, we put a man on the moon. Can you imagine the millions of man-hours that went into preparing for that, and all of the money, and all of the danger? Do you know what we didn't have to spend money on? We didn't spend one man-hour wondering if the moon would be there when we got there. What a testimony to the consistency and control of God's creation.

The moon was right where God put it, and the Lord that created and controls it, that Lord blessed the promise.

You see, when you're in the dark period of your life—when you don't know how, when, where, why, you don't know—yet you bless the Lord, worship, stay faithful, and encourage others, God will in turn bless you. The God that controls the universe. He's still in charge, by the way, and He will bless you.

But notice the place. He will bless thee out of Zion. That's Jerusalem. That's the temple. That's where God's presence was manifested in the tabernacle and then in the temple of Solomon.

God's presence and God's blessings are related to a place. If you are in the place of blessing, God will bless you. I learned years ago that getting things from God is easy. Getting in the position to get them is what's hard. It's being in a right relationship with God where you get the blessings of God. So bless the Lord, stand, stay faithful, encourage others, and God will bless you.

Have you ever worked at midnight and been eager for the daylight to come? I've been there and done that. All night long at a Texaco service station in Chattanooga, I would work, and I would literally stand on my tiptoes, put my finger up against the wall to balance myself to keep from falling asleep. When the first sunlight was coming over Missionary Ridge, I knew it was almost time for me to get off work. If you're in the night, in the dark, do you know that the dark and the night end?

And there shall be no more curse: but the throne of God and of the Lamb shall be in it; and his servants shall serve him: And they shall see his face; and his name shall be in their foreheads. And there shall be no night there. — Revelation 22:3

There will be no night there, no times of darkness and wandering, of not seeing clearly, of not being able to see far off, of not being aware of danger. There will be no night there, no danger.

...and they need no candle, neither light of the sun; for the Lord God giveth them light: and they shall reign for ever and ever. — *Revelation 22:5*

The morning is coming. It's coming for all of us. Having a desire to depart and to be with Christ which is far better, nevertheless to remain with you is more needful—and there's that dynamic tension. In your life when it gets dark, He that keepeth Israel shall never slumber nor sleep. God is awake in the night, in your night. God is watching. God is protecting. God is providing. The morning comes, and the sun is coming up. There will be no night there. When I read such promises and think about it, my heart cries out like John at the end of that last chapter, "Come, Lord Jesus." AMEN!

Chapter Two

Be Still and Know
Psalm 46

Be Still and Know
Psalm 46

A fellow came into a crowded waiting room at a doctor's office. He walked over to the window where the receptionist was. She opened the window and asked, "What can I do for you?" He said, "I've got shingles." And she said, "Okay, just take a seat, the doctor will be with you eventually." He waited a long time before finally walking up and asking, "Lady, would you tell me where he wants me to put these shingles for the roof?"

What she thought and what he wanted were totally different things. She thought he was sick, but he just wanted to deliver shingles for the new roof. I think that that is sometimes the way we preachers are. We think we know what people need, and what they want. But we may be way off base. We must trust the Lord to direct us to what people need.

Recently, the Lord directed my attention to this 46th Psalm. I was listening to a friend of mine preach on a CD. He was not preaching on this Psalm or even on this subject, but in the middle of his sermon, he quoted, *"Be still and know that I am God."* (Psalm 46:10) And I could not get away from that fact.

It strikes me that being still, whatever that means, is tied to knowledge. *"Be still and know that I am God."* What you know, as a believer, ought to be able to cause you to be still. To be still doesn't mean to be idle. It doesn't mean to be lazy or inert, to just sit around and twiddle your spiritual thumbs. Instead, being still has the idea of not being anxiety-ridden or upset. It means to be quiet, to be restful in spirit.

In Psalm 46, the first verse and the last verse are very much alike.

God is our refuge and strength, a very present help in trouble. — Psalm 46:1

The Lord of hosts is with us; the God of Jacob is our refuge. Selah. — Psalm 46:11

The word 'selah' occurs at the end of verse 3, again at the end of verse 7, and then, unlike most Psalms, after the last verse. This is unusual. You would expect this Psalm, to have a 'selah' after verse 3 and verse 7, but it is kind of surprising that there is also one listed at the end of the Psalm.

In a world where everything is topsy-turvy, it is so easy for us to become that way ourselves. Most people are uneasy.

God is our refuge and strength, a very present help in trouble. Therefore will not we fear, though the earth be removed, and though the mountains be carried into the midst of the sea; Though the waters thereof roar and be troubled, though the mountains shake with the swelling thereof. Selah. — Psalm 46:1-3

Think about what you've read. The word 'selah' is a musical rest. It means 'to pause, to think, to consider, to muse, to meditate' on what you've just read, what you've just sung, or what you've just heard sung. There are rests in music—notes and rests. There is no music in the rest, but the rest is still a part of the music. When you read the music—not the words, but the music—the words don't say "rest;" but there is a little sign in those five lines and four spaces that means "rest." I think God's people need the knowledge of rest. "Be still and know."

There is a river, the streams whereof shall make glad the city of God, the holy place of the tabernacles of the most High. God is in the midst of her; she shall not be moved: God shall help her, and that right early. — Psalm 46:4-5

In these verses, the psalmist is talking about this people, this city of God, and the idea in the Hebrew is "first thing in the morning." God will help His people first thing in the morning, "right early."

The heathen raged, the kingdoms were moved: he uttered his voice, the earth melted. The Lord of hosts is with us; the God of Jacob is our refuge. Selah. — Psalm 46:6-7

This is the second time God is mentioned as our refuge, first in verse 1 and now here in verse 7. It will be mentioned again in verse 11. Selah, think about that.

These first seven verses are the words of the psalmist, but in verses 8-10, God is speaking.

Come, behold the works of the Lord, what desolations he hath made in the earth. He maketh wars to cease unto the end of the earth; he breaketh the bow, and cutteth the spear in sunder; he burneth the chariot in the fire. Be still, and know that I am God: I will be exalted among the heathen, I will be exalted in the earth. — Psalm 46:8-10

The word for "heathen" is the source for our word for "Gentile." Verse 11, then, is the final reassertion of his faith and trust in God when he says, "The Lord of hosts is with us; the God of Jacob is our refuge. Selah."

The Reality

Though the earth be removed, and though the mountains be carried into the midst of the sea; Though the waters thereof roar and be troubled, though the mountains shake with the swelling thereof. — Psalm 46:2-3

When I read those verses, I'm reminded of earthquakes, volcanic eruptions, hurricanes, tsunamis. "Though the earth be removed"—that is an earthquake. "Though the mountains be carried into the midst of the sea"—that is a volcanic eruption.

"Though the waters thereof roar"—that is a hurricane. "Though the mountains shake with the swelling thereof"—that is a tsunami. Think about it. What the psalmist has identified are four major natural disasters. Isn't it odd that nature should, by itself, bring disasters?

We forget that the Bible says that "the whole of creation groaneth and prevaileth together in pain until now...waiting for the manifestation of the sons of God." (Romans 8:22, 19) So when there are natural disasters, when nature is acting unnaturally, it is the whole creation groaning under the curse of sin, waiting for its redemption, for the manifestation of the sons of God.

But there are other disasters that are not just physical disasters. There are emotional storms. There are difficulties economically. There are difficult times politically and tough times around the world militarily, not to mention the problems of decaying morality. Wherever you look there are problems.

That is the reality. It doesn't matter whether you are a democrat or a republican, wherever you look there are difficulties.

The Resolve

Here is the most amazing statement in verse two: "We will not fear." That is the resolve that the psalmist expresses, in spite of the reality of difficulties. When our difficulties become so bad that the mountains roll down into the sea and the sea roars, we have decided we will not fear. I read that, and it is astounding. Here comes a looming disaster, and you are able to stand there saying, "But we won't be afraid."

The word "fear" does not mean that we won't be startled or surprised, that we won't jump when there is a loud boom. We are going to react, but we are not going to be characterized by fear. We are not going to be governed by fear. We are not going to live in a lifestyle of fear. We are going to be still. The opposite of fear is to be still. I mentioned earlier that being still, quiet, at rest, is tied to knowledge. Here it is in verse 10: "Be still and know that He is God." The knowledge is the reason you can be without fear.

You might say, "Well there is so much I don't know. I don't know what is going to happen to the economy. I don't know about this and that," you might say. Yes, **but you do not let what you don't know upset what you do know. And you do not let what you know be upset by what you don't know.**

The reason the psalmist is able to say "we won't fear" is because of what he knows. The reality is that this is a tough time, a bad situation. The resolve is that we are not going to live a lifestyle of fear. How can he say that? Because of what he knows. What does he know?

Verse 1: God is...
Verse 5: God is...
Verse 7: The Lord of hosts is... the God of Jacob is...
Verse 10: ...know that I am God: I will be exalted...
Verse 11: The Lord of hosts is... the God of Jacob is...

The Bible says, "He that cometh to God must believe that He is and that He is the rewarder of them that diligently seek Him." (Hebrews 11:6) Do you ever thank God for the fact that He is? A little boy was saying his good night prayers. When he finished his prayers for Mom and Daddy, the dog, the cat, and everybody else, he said, "And God please take care of Yourself. Because if something happened to You, we'd all be in a terrible mess." He is right. God is. Not that God was, not that God will be—God is eternal, present tense. God is.

God is our refuge; the psalmist repeats this three times in verse 1, verse 7, and verse 11. What is a refuge? A refuge is a place of safety. "The Lord is our rock, in Him we hide, a shelter in the time of storm," the hymn says. But God is not only our safety; verse 1 says He is "a very present help in trouble." Would it not have been sufficient if he had said, "God is a help"? But the psalmist adds not one, but two modifiers to add intensity —"very present." In our trouble, God is very present. We sometimes say, "Oh God, come and help us." God is here. "Oh God, come and bless us." God is here. He is a very present (intensified) very present help.

The person who says, "Where is God?" is spiritually blind. God is. God is not just help, but a very present help. One word in the New Testament for the Holy Spirit is "Comforter." Jesus said to His disciples, "I will send you another comforter, that He will abide with you forever." (John 14:16) The word "another" doesn't mean another of a different kind, but it means another of the same kind. The word we translate in our Bible as "comforter" is literally a word that means "one who is called and comes alongside to help." We will not fear! God is. God is our help, our refuge. Verse 1 also says He is our strength. Not only our refuge and safety, but our strength! That is our power in the time of trouble.

A while back, I was thinking about the three Hebrews who were thrown into the furnace of fire. You remember those? When the king looked in he saw four, and he said, "The fourth one is like to the Son of God." The Bible doesn't say that the three Hebrews saw the fourth man when they were in the fire. But they weren't being burned. They knew their clothes were not singed. The ropes were burned, and they were loose and walking around. The Bible doesn't say that they saw the Lord was in there with them. A lot of times, we don't see the Lord. We don't sense His presence, but the Lord is our strength, our refuge, our help.

The words of the hymn say: "I've seen the lightning flashing, and I've heard the thunder roll, I've felt sins breakers dashing, trying to conquer my soul, but I've heard the voice of Jesus telling me still to fight on; I've promised to never leave you, never to leave you alone." God is. God is our refuge and safety. God is our strength. God is our help in time of trouble.

But he goes beyond that, God is with us. If He is our strength, present in trouble, then He is with us! He is with us in the present. In verse 5, He is in the midst. In verse 7, He is the Lord of hosts. He is with us. Whenever God is being described as being the "The Lord of Hosts," the word "hosts" is referring to an army; it is a military term. He is the Lord of an army. Hey troubled, worried, ill at ease, unrestful Christian in an upside down world, God and His armies are with us. And if God be for us, who could be against us? The Lord of hosts is with us! Verse 11, the psalmist repeats, "The Lord of hosts is with us."

The Supply

The psalm starts with all of this upheaval, the most horrible disasters that the psalmist can imagine—from the hurricane, the tsunami, the earthquake, the volcanic eruptions, the worst things that could happen in that world. We think of it as the worst things that could happen in our world, outside of our control. But verse 4 is different. Sure, there is upset, and the world is upside down; but there is a river. Not a stormy sea, not a hurricane, but there is a river. That is our supply.

Look at the cities of the world. The majority of the big cities of the world are built on the banks of rivers—the river Thames in London, the river Nile in Egypt, and many of our early cities in this country. The river is the source of our supply, and God is saying to us, "Yeah, things are in a mess, physically, emotionally, politically. Tornadoes, earthquakes, tsunamis, hurricanes—everything is whirling around you, but stop a minute. There is a river. It is not rushing, and it is not stagnant; it just keeps coming, and that is the supply. My grace is sufficient."

In the words of the song, "Just when I need Him, Jesus is near. Just when I falter, just when I fear. Ready to help me, ready to cheer. Just when I need Him most." Haven't you found that to be true? There is a river. That is the supply. "My God shall supply all you need according to His riches and glory by Christ Jesus." (Philippians 4:19) There is a river.

The Sovereign Rule

So, if that's not enough that God is **our safety, our strength, our source, and our supply, God is also sovereign.** In verse 8, God is saying, "Come and look at what I've already done."

Come, behold the works of the Lord, what desolations he hath made (past tense) in the earth.— Psalm 46:8

Come and see; behold His works. He is a sovereign God. In verse 9, God is even looking at the future and saying that He will make wars to cease unto the end of the earth. How is He going to do that? Is God going to say to the rulers of this world, "Come on boys, play nice with each other," and they say, "Okay, we'll do that"? No, He's going to conquer them. The way He is going to stop all wars is to destroy the implements. He said He breaks the bow, He cuts the spear, and burns the chariots. Arrows, spears, chariots, horses—this was the military of that day; and God said, "I'm going to destroy." He's going to destroy the possibility of war. When King Jesus rules this earth in Jerusalem, He will rule with a rod of iron. Righteousness and justice are ahead of us because He is sovereign.

There was a time when one of my close friends in the ministry had a terrible battle with Crohn's disease, a terrible battle. At the same time, his wife had shingles that settled in her eye. It was bad! Then, another of my preacher friends had been told that he was going to die. He was my age at the time. Another of my preacher friends in his 80s rides in a little scooter from his house next door to the church and preaches from a wheelchair or from that scooter; he's still pastoring. While yet another of my preacher friends, his wife was scheduled to have surgery to fuse three bones in her neck. She'd had surgery on her back just two months before. But the day before her operation, he came down with the flu. Isn't that wonderful timing? It was one thing after the other for this couple. She has Lupus and all kinds of problems. And now, he had gotten ill with the flu when she was to be operated on at 9:00 the next morning. God, what are You doing? We're bound to ask that. "Be still." Cool it. Stifle yourself. God is in control.

You may say, "I just don't know what is going to happen." Oh yes, you do. The Lord is going to come. Suddenly, but certainly, and the dead in Christ are going to be raised. And we who remain will be called up together with them in the clouds to meet the Lord in the air, and we will forever be with the Lord.

If you think it is rough now, you wait until the Church of Jesus Christ is gone, and seven years of hell on earth begin. The Lord is going to come back. He is going to establish His Kingdom. We won't study war anymore; it will be peace. Not just peace in the valley, but peace on the mountaintop. Not just the Jews, but the Gentiles as well. We are going to enter into that. He is sovereign.

Be still. Know. Know your God. Know who He is. Know what He has done. Know what He is doing. Know what He is going to do. What does God say? He said, "I'm going to be exalted." The day will come when every knee will bow, every tongue will confess that Jesus Christ is Lord to the glory of God the Father. He's going to be exalted.

Just be still and know. AMEN!

Chapter Three

Essentials for Effectiveness
Zechariah 4

Essentials for Effectiveness
Zechariah 4

If you would think back through the months or years to the point of your conversion, have you accomplished for the Lord what you thought you would accomplish by this point in your Christian life? The truth is, for the most part, we haven't; we are largely ineffective. Yet, I would assume, we all want to be more effective. There has to be some dissatisfaction with our spiritual progress. In fact, a Christian who has become satisfied with a spiritual plateau has already begun the process of backsliding. And, I think, we have reason to question any person who professes to be saved and does not desire to be more effective for the Lord. What is necessary to be effective? What does it take to be effective as a Christian, as a church, or as a family? What will make us effective for the Lord?

Well, the answer to becoming more effective can be found in the prophet Zechariah's vision.

And [an angel] said unto me, What seest thou? And I said, I have looked, and behold a candlestick all of gold, with a bowl upon the top of it, and his seven lamps thereon, and seven pipes to the seven lamps, which are upon the top thereof: And two olive trees by it, one upon the right side of the bowl, and the other upon the left side thereof. — *Zechariah 4:2-3*

That is some vision. First, Zechariah sees a candlestick, a menorah. You can often see these around the Christmas season; as Christians observe Christmas, Jews will observe Hanukkah. The menorah is the national symbol of the nation of Israel. The menorah was the candlestick in the tabernacle and later in the temple. It is an elaborate instrument. In souvenir shops, you can buy one for as little as $5 or as much as $500 depending on the size and the quality.

The candlestick that is set in the tabernacle and later in the temple had to be a large one, perhaps as high as the height of a man. Coming up from the base, it had one cylinder, and on the top of it was a lamp stand, a place for a candle, and then beside it on either side was a candlestick. That makes three. Beside each of them, farther out, there is another on either side. That makes five. Beside each of those two, you have yet two more. That makes seven. In all, you have a center cylinder, three on the right, and three on the left, and all of them are attached to this one base.

This is similar to what Zechariah saw, only the one that he saw also had a bowl at the top of it. In that bowl was olive oil. From this bowl, there were pipes, tubes, or hoses that ran down to the base of each of these seven candlesticks. The wick was inserted down into that bowl at the base of each candlestick. The oil, then, would work itself up the wick and burn.

This candlestick or menorah was a very impressive thing, all made of gold. Now, we are told nothing here about the mining of the gold, but somebody had to mine it. We are told nothing here about smelting, chemistry, carpentry, metallurgy, or geometry. We are told nothing here about all of the processes, but there is a tremendous process that has gone into fashioning this beautiful candelabra, this menorah made all of gold. But though it was impressive, it was lifeless, not dead but lifeless. It had no life.

Zechariah also saw two olive trees standing on either side of this beautiful candlestick. Although the candlestick was mechanical and lifeless, the olive trees were not. They were alive. Just as nothing is said about the process or shaping of the menorah, neither are we given any word about how these olive trees bear olives or how that oil flows from these olive trees into the big bowl at the top of the menorah. We are given nothing of the process, but the process was an arduous one. Somebody had to pick the olives, and somebody had to press the olives, crush them, and pour the oil into the bowl. All of this picking and pressing and pouring— all of it has to be done in order to get the oil from the olive trees into the big bowl at the top where it will then flow by gravity into each of these little reservoirs.

And I answered again, and said unto him, What be these two olive branches which through the two golden pipes empty the golden oil out of themselves? And he answered me and said, Knowest thou not what these be? And I said, No, my lord. — Zechariah 4:12-13

The mechanical, lifeless candlestick must be continually supplied with oil from these two live olive trees. Without it, the candlestick is of no value and has no use. This candlestick, as beautiful as it is, becomes useless. It becomes a mockery, a shallow, hollow, vain, caricature of what it ought to be. It becomes nothing. The value of the candlestick is the light, not its beauty. In order for the candlestick to function, it must depend upon the continual supply of the oil. If there is not that continual supply of the oil then when you light the wick, it will burn but a moment, sputter out, and die. Do you see? The mechanical and lifeless is dependent on the flow from the living.

Whatever institution or organization you want to talk about is like the candlestick. It is lifeless and all mechanical. In America, you cannot think of a church without thinking of a building. The church building is like the candlestick. Although the building may be beautiful with the stained glass windows, all of it is mechanical. You cannot say it is dead; it is just lifeless. It has never had life. It is inanimate. It has of itself no life at all.

Like the candlestick, the church or the Christian service organization of any kind has to be dependent upon something that has life in order for it to fulfill its purpose. If the local church, the denomination, the Christian institution, or service organization of whatever kind is to function, it has to be dependent upon something that has life. In this instance, the candlestick has to depend upon the life that is in the olive trees to get the oil to it, or else it cannot burn.

Verse 12 says that these two olive trees empty out of themselves the oil that goes into this golden candlestick. The golden candlestick has to have a continual supply of oil coming from the olive trees to the big reservoir at the top, through the seven hoses, tubes, or pipes, to the base of each of those lamp stands where the wick is lit. It has to be continually supplied.

That means then, that in order for the inanimate, lifeless to function, to fulfill its use and the purpose for which it was created, that inanimate, lifeless organization has to be dependent upon life from some source outside of itself; and that life source has to be ongoing. For all of its weaknesses, for all of its divisiveness, for all of its apathy, for all of its carnality, for all of its immaturity, the Church of the Lord Jesus Christ is the agency through whom God is working in this day.

To the intent that now unto the principalities and powers in heavenly places might be known by the church the manifold wisdom of God, — Ephesians 3:10
Unto him be glory in the church by Christ Jesus throughout all ages, world without end. Amen. — Ephesians 3:21

It is not through nature that man learns the manifold wisdom of God. It is through the church. The church, then, must be dependent upon this life-giving source. So how is it going to work?

So I answered and spake to the angel that talked with me, saying, What are these, my lord? Then the angel that talked with me answered and said unto me, Knowest thou not what these be? And I said, No, my lord. Then he answered and spake unto me, saying, This is the word of the LORD unto Zerubbabel, saying, Not by might, nor by power, but by my spirit, saith the LORD of hosts. Who art thou, O great mountain? before Zerubbabel thou shalt become a plain: and he shall bring forth the headstone thereof with shoutings, crying, Grace, grace unto it. —Zechariah 4:4-7

The hands of Zerubbabel have laid the foundation of this house; his hands shall also finish it; and thou shalt know that the LORD of hosts hath sent me unto you.— Zechariah 4:9

Here is this great obstacle before Zechariah, "O great mountain." And what happens to the obstacle? It becomes a plain, and Zechariah is going to finish the building. He is going to put on the headstone or the capstone shouting and crying, "Grace, grace unto it." Now how is he going to do that? Well, I will give you a couple of negatives, it is not by might nor by power, and one positive, "but by my Spirit, saith the Lord of hosts."

What is essential, then, to making us effective? How are we going to work if we are the inanimate light stand, and how do we get the life-giving oil to make our lights shine? How are we going to fulfill our purpose? In the same way that Zechariah finished his building—it is "not by might, nor by power, but by my Spirit, saith the Lord of hosts."

Not by Might

The word "might" means strength of moral character. Isn't that amazing? In fact, I was shocked when I looked it up and found in Proverbs 31, where it talks about the virtuous woman, the word that is translated "virtuous" is the same word that is translated here "might." Really, it is the same word! It does not mean just sexually pure. It is broader than that. It speaks of good moral character. That woman in Proverbs 31 is a strong woman.

"Not by might." Wait a minute. We have to have good character. So, I am not saying that we ought not to emphasize godly living. Good character is essential, but just good character alone is not going to get the work done. I wish we would learn that. We are not going to be able to do God's work without good moral character, but just having good moral character and the strength of it—that alone—is not going to make us effective.

Whenever you judge your spirituality based upon what you do or do not do, you really make a mistake. You think you are spiritual because you don't do this, don't do that, or don't do the other. When you judge yourself on the negatives, what you do or not do, you have made a big mistake, because a dead man in a graveyard does not do those things either. For every good and moral Christian, I can show you a good and moral unbeliever.

You are not going to accomplish the work of God effectively apart from good moral character. But just having good moral character is not going to make you effective. It is not going to be by might or strength of moral character.

Nor by Power

Then God goes on to say, "Not by might, nor by power." What does that mean? Muscle. You see, not by might is what you are inwardly. Nor by power is what you are outwardly--not by moral character and not by muscle strength. What is He saying? He is actually saying that this temple that Zerubbabel is going to build—God will finish it. God started it, and God will finish it. It is not going to be finished solely with muscle.

We talk about Christians needing to work hard for the Lord, needing to be faithful and dedicated. I am all for that, but just that effort alone is not going to make you effective. It is not going to get the job done. Nobody is going to be an effective Christian based solely on good character and hard work.

By my Spirit

One of the symbols of the Holy Spirit is oil. When kings were anointed, it was with oil, a symbol of the Holy Spirit. When priests were anointed, it was with oil, a symbol of the Holy Spirit. When prophets were anointed, it was with oil, a symbol of the Holy Spirit. It is even said of our Lord, "Thou hast anointed thee with the oil of gladness above all thy fellows." (Psalm 45:7 and Heb. 1:9) It is essential that there be that enduement of Holy Spirit power.

Now, dear friend, there is a vast difference between being indwelt by the Holy Spirit and being empowered by the Holy Spirit. There is a difference between the indwelling, residing

Holy Spirit and the infilling, presiding Holy Spirit. Good character and moral character, noble as it is and needed as it is, is not a guarantee of effectiveness. Hard work and dedicated labor is not a guarantee of effectiveness. There must be that presiding oil of the Holy Spirit that controls you.

Rather than thinking of possessing the Holy Spirit, learn to think of the Holy Spirit possessing you. There is a vast difference. For you see, the oil in the bowl flowing through those tubes through the seven different stands has to continue to flow. The candlestick is lifeless, inanimate, and has no life of its own. All mechanics, beautiful as they are and impressive as they may be, are of no value without the life of that oil continually flowing through it.

The process that fashioned the candlestick has to happen in my life and your life. You say, "What do you mean?" I mean, if you want a candlestick that is ready to receive the oil, there has to be a mining, a smelting, a forming, a beating, and a shaping. It is a long, hard, slow, arduous, toilsome, and painful process. You do not take a candlestick and make it overnight, and neither do you become a mature Christian overnight.

If it is the Spirit that enables Zerubbabel to lay the foundation, and it is the Spirit that will enable him to finish it and put the headstone on it. Then what is the process for us? Let me suggest to you that it is basically the same as the process of getting that oil from the olive to the bowl. There has to be picking, pressing, and pouring. That is a process that does not happen overnight. It does not happen without effort, even painful effort.

There are three steps to this process.

A. There must be a total, complete admittance of our own inability.

That is hard for us, for we are raised in a culture from day one that says, "Study, work hard, and be successful." We have been taught from day one to be self-reliant. We are taught to become self-controlled, self-confident, and self-conscious, not in a negative way, but conscious of ourselves as distinct from others of our abilities. The little train that said: "I think I can, I think I can, I think I can." He goes down the other side saying: "I knew I could, I knew I could, I knew I could." That is the way we are programmed, but if you bring that secular thinking into Christianity, friend, it does not work. Instead, you must to come to the place where you can say:

For I know that in me (that is, in my flesh,) dwelleth no good thing. — Romans 7:18

Our whole society would preclude us from coming to that conclusion. Do you think our Lord knew what He was talking about when He said to His disciples, "Without me, ye can do nothing?" (John 15:5)

Do you think He is telling the truth, or do you think He is just stretching it? "But wait a minute," you say, "I have abilities, I have brains, and I have physical strength. I have talents, I can sing, I can play, I can preach, I can teach. I can clean the church building, I can cut the grass, I can do this, and I can do that." But Jesus says, "Without me, ye can do nothing." Go right on doing it your way, but when it is all said and done, all that effort is nothing.

In the hymn "Rock of Ages," we sing: "In my hand no price I bring, simply to the cross I cling." You must come to the place where Paul came, "Within me, that is within my flesh, dwelleth no good thing?" (Romans 7:18) Now, that is a hard place for us to come, but that is where we must come. If you don't come to this first step, the other two steps will never be attained. If you can come to this place, then the other two steps are possible.

B. There must be a continual enduement or anointing of the Spirit.

The continual flowing of the oil from out of the olive trees into the big bowl and from the bowl through the hoses, tubes, and pipes into the seven wicks has to be a process that comes by continual asking. If you want the continual flow of the Holy Spirit, there has to be a continual asking.

And he said unto them, Which of you shall have a friend, and shall go unto him at midnight, and say unto him, Friend, lend me three loaves; For a friend of mine in his journey is come to me, and I have nothing to set before him? And he from within shall answer and say, Trouble me not: the door is now shut, and my children are with me in bed; I cannot rise and give thee. I say unto you, Though he will not rise and give him, because he is his friend, yet because of his importunity he will rise and give him as many as he needeth.
— Luke 11:5-8

This friend just keeps on asking. Let me give you my translation:

And I say unto you, [continue to] Ask, and it shall be [continually] given you; [continue to] seek, and ye shall [continue to] find; [continue to] knock, and it shall [continue to] be opened unto you. For every one that [continually] asketh [continually] receiveth; and he that [continually] seeketh [continually] findeth; and to him that [continually] knocketh it shall be [continually] opened. If a son shall ask bread of any of you that is a father, will he give him a stone? or if he ask a fish, will he for a fish give him a serpent? Or if he shall ask an egg, will he offer him a scorpion? If ye then, being evil, know how to give good gifts unto your children: how much more shall your heavenly Father give the Holy Spirit to them that ask him? — Luke11:9-13

If you want the continual enduement—the continual flowing of the oil—and the power of the Holy Spirit, there has to be first a complete admittance of your own total inability. Second, there has to be a continual asking. You cannot have today's enduement based on yesterday's asking. There are so many people who are trying to live today successfully in the power of yesterday, last week, last month, last year, or ten years ago, and you cannot do it. You cannot do it. Maybe one reason we have so little power is because we ask for it so little.

C. There must be a continual or consistent appropriation by faith.

Most people who are asking for the filling of the Spirit do not really want the filling of the Spirit; they want the feeling of the Spirit. If I were to ask you if you are filled with the Holy Spirit right now, would you say: "Oh, mercy. I do not feel cold chills running up and down my body. I am not weeping with joy. I am not shouting 'Glory Hallelujah,' so I must not be Spirit filled." No, you are confusing *feelings* and *filling*.

If you were to ask me, "Brother Mathews, are you filled with the Spirit right now?" In all honesty I would tell you, yes. That is not presumptuous; that is honest. How can I say that? Because I have sought the face of God. It is in His providence that He directed me to this passage of Scripture. In His power and for His glory, I preach the Word. That is what Spirit-filling is. It is the controlling of the Spirit of God.

How do you have the controlling of the Spirit? You get it by faith. You do not have it by feelings, you have it by faith. "I don't know if I have enough faith," you may think. But it takes more faith to be saved than it does to be Spirit-filled. Think about it. It takes a lot of faith for you to say, "I want Jesus to come into my heart." You got saved by faith, didn't you? If you had feelings, praise God. The feelings come after the faith. You do not base your salvation on your feelings, but on faith. You do not put your faith in the feelings. You put your faith in the facts.

For whosoever shall call upon the name of the Lord shall be saved. — Romans 10:13

One last question from our passage in Zechariah: who are these olive trees? That is you. That is I. For you see, the church, the rescue mission, the orphanage, the Christian school, the Bible College, the mission board—all these are just mechanics. It is lifeless apart from the life, the oil of the Holy Spirit, that flows out of us giving life to the mechanisms. It has to be "not by might, nor by power, but by my Spirit, saith the Lord of Hosts." AMEN!

Chapter Four

In Bondage? Look Up!
Ezekiel 1

In Bondage? Look Up!
Ezekiel 1

Now it came to pass in the thirtieth year, in the fourth month, in the fifth day of the month, as I was among the captives by the river of Chebar, that the heavens were opened, and I saw visions of God. In the fifth day of the month, which was the fifth year of king Jehoiachin's captivity. — Ezekiel 1:1-2

The Babylonians, also called Chaldeans under the rule of Nebuchadnezzar, made three different raids into Israel and Jerusalem. They came in 605 BC and took some captives. They came again in 597 BC, and it was then that they took some of the goodliest young men of the Jews among whom was Daniel and his three friends whom we know as the three Hebrew children. Among those captives was this young priest by the name of Ezekiel. Ezekiel's name means God strengthens. He was a priest in Jerusalem. It was only when he became a prisoner of war, if you will, in Babylon, that God called him to be a prophet, and we have this book.

His book is a long one, 48 chapters. Let me summarize the whole book in four statements, and if you get these you'll have a basic understanding of the book of Ezekiel. **One, the temple will be destroyed. Two, the temple will be rebuilt. Three, Israel will be scattered. Four, Israel will be re-gathered.** And if you get those four statements, you've got a basic understanding of the book. The temple was destroyed on the third invasion of Israel in 586 BC. Not only was the temple destroyed but all of the riches of the temple were taken into Babylon. So he is writing telling them what will happen. It did happen, and he's telling them the temple will be rebuilt. He's saying, "You will be scattered." He's saying this about 11 years before it happened, and then after it happened he writes and says, "But you will be gathered."

And he said unto me, Son of man, stand upon thy feet, and I will speak unto thee. And the spirit entered into me when he spake unto me, and set me upon my feet, that I heard him that spake unto me. And he said unto me, Son of man, I send thee to the children of Israel. — Ezekiel 2:1-3

There are phrases that occur over, and over, and over throughout the book of Ezekiel. For example, the phrases **Thus saith the Lord** or **The hand of the LORD** or **The Word of the Lord** or **The Spirit of the LORD**. No less than 63 times in these 48 chapters is this phrase stated: **That they may know that I am the LORD**. The title he uses in Ezekiel 2:1, "And he said unto me, Son of Man," that title appears 94 times in this book. It literally is "Son of Adam."

This first chapter of Ezekiel is one of the most mystifying, intriguing sections of the Scripture. It's the section where **Ezekiel saw his vision.** Verse 4 through verse 14, he has the **vision of these cherubim,** angelic-like creatures with four faces and four wings. Then in verse 15 and following, he has the **vision of the chariot,** and in verse 26 the **vision of the throne** and the man who sits on the throne. Then, in verse 28 of chapter 1, Ezekiel gives us his concluding statement about all that he had seen.

As the appearance of the bow that is in the cloud in the day of rain, so was the appearance of the brightness round about. This was the appearance of the likeness of the glory of the LORD. And when I saw it, I fell upon my face, and I heard a voice of one that spake. — Ezekiel 1:28

Clearly, the book of Ezekiel is inspired Scripture: "For the prophecy came not in old time by the will of man: but holy men of God spake as they were moved by the Holy Ghost." (2 Peter 1:21) But it appears to me, humanly speaking, that Ezekiel had a difficult time explaining the vision. If you read the first chapter, you see no less than 15 times the word like or likeness. The word as appears 10 times, and the word appearance is used 10 times. It's as though Ezekiel had difficulty describing everything that he had seen. And if you start reading in verse 4 and read through the end of the first chapter, your head would be spinning. It is one of the strangest passages in all of the word of God.

In the first part of this chapter 1, he has a **vision of God;** in the last part of chapter 1, he hears the **voice of God;** and in the first part of chapter 2, he is given the **vocation from God.** Chapter 1 is his encounter of God, chapter 2:1-3 is **his encounter with God,** and then the remaining verses of chapter 2 is an **encounter for God.** The focus of this first chapter is on the glory of God.

You are Not Exempt From Difficulty

Now it came to pass in the thirtieth year, in the fourth month, in the fifth day of the month, as I was among the captives by the river of Chebar, that the heavens were opened, and I saw visions of God. In the fifth day of the month, which was the fifth year of king Jehoiachin's captivity. — Ezekiel 1:1-2

I wish to be very practical here, and the first thing I want you to know is this: being righteous, being right with God, does not exempt you from experiencing great difficulty. We need to hear that. Did you catch it in verse 1? "I was among the captives by the river of Chebar." The river Chebar is actually now a canal about 200 miles north-northwest of the city of Babylon, near the city where Saddam Hussein reigned. That water flows into the river Tigris and then joins with the Euphrates. Here is a man who was right with God and yet was taken captive.

If you would believe the televangelists today, you should never have difficulty if you've got faith. God wants you healthy and wealthy; and if you're neither of those, then it's because you don't have faith in God, you're not right with God, or you've got sin in your life. Those people have done great harm to average Christians. You'd be amazed at the mail that I get. I received a letter from an 87-year-old lady who, after 60-some years as a member of a good Baptist church, was not sure now that she was saved because she was having health problems. She was watching these idiots on television who tell her that if you're right with God, God would heal you, just like that. And she's doubting her own salvation because she's been watching programs that are not biblical to begin with, programs designed to get money out of people.

Listen, you can be right with God and experience great difficulty. You need to remember that. Did Abel who was righteous deserve to be killed by his brother Cain? No, but he was. Did Joseph deserve to be sold into slavery in Egypt? No, but he was. Did Shadrach, Meshach, and Abednego deserve to be thrown into a fiery furnace? No, but they were. Did Daniel deserve to be thrown into a den of lions? No, but he was. Did Joshua and Caleb deserve to wait 40 years to go into the land of Canaan? No, but they did. Did the apostle Paul deserve the persecution that he encountered, afloat in the Mediterranean, three times beaten with rods, stoned and left for dead? Did Paul deserve that? No, and the list goes on and on. Yet the mentality of Christianity today is not Christ-focused but people-focused, and that's the wrong focus.

"All they that live godly in Christ Jesus will suffer persecution." (2 Timothy 3:12) What the Bible says is exactly the opposite of what is being preached today. Being right with God doesn't exempt you from experiencing great difficulty. Not only is the Bible replete with such examples, but history itself is. Fanny Crosby authored such songs as Blessed assurance, Jesus is mine. Did Fanny Crosby deserve to be blinded by a mistaken doctor when she was 6 weeks of age and live a life past 90 in blindness? No, but she was.

You read the poems of Annie Johnson Flint, some of which have been put to music: "He giveth more grace when the burdens go greater. He giveth more strength when our strength is gone. To added afflictions He addeth His mercy, to multiplied trials, His multiplied peace." Did Annie Johnson Flint deserve to be so disabled by arthritis that she was bed-fast and eventually blinded by diabetes? No, but she was. She would lie in pain at night, but refuse to take the pain pills that would make her loopy and not be able to think. In her mind, she would write these beautiful poems again and again, memorizing them in her mind without ever putting a word on paper. When her caretaker came in the morning to wake her and give her food and change her— she had to have somebody 24 hours around the clock— then Annie would say, "Get your paper and write this down."

Being right with God doesn't mean that you've got it easy, and that is so hard for us to accept because whenever it happens that we have difficulty, we think, "Nobody knows the trouble I've seen." Yeah, we do! The first statement is that being right with God does not exempt us from experiencing great difficulty.

Your Circumstances are Not Unique to You

The second lesson we learn is that what may be happening to any one of us is not unique to us. Did you catch it? Verse 1 said, "I was AMONG the captives." You think, "Nobody knows my problem." Yes, everyone does. The Bible says, "There hath no temptation taken you but such as is common to man." (1 Corinthians 10:13)

We all have difficulties, and our tendency is to say, "Why me?" instead of saying, "Why not me?" And instead of focusing on why this is happening, maybe we ought to be focusing on, "What do You want to teach me, Lord? What do You want me to demonstrate to others through this affliction that has come upon me?" Have you contemplated 2 Corinthians 1: 3-5? "That the God of all comfort has comforted us, that we in turn may be a comfort to others."

Back in 1990, I woke up early one morning about 4:00 or 5:00 and knew something was wrong. Before I walked to the mirror, I knew I had Bell's Palsy. The whole side of my face was frozen. Why did this happen? I was in the middle of revival meetings, preaching in churches. I was in his office at 9:00 when the doctor arrived. The nurse asked, "Do you have an appointment?"

I said, "No, I've got something worse than that. I've got Bell's Palsy." They loaded me down with Prednisone and said, "Surely you're not going to preach tonight." "Oh yeah, I'm going to go, and I'm going to preach," I answered. I used a handkerchief when I needed to say a word that you had to pop, like a P or a B. I just pushed through with the handkerchief. I drooled for three weeks and preached for three weeks. And then it cleared up. Why did this happen to me? I didn't know. But about four years later the phone rang and a preacher friend of mine said, "I've got Bell's Palsy." I was able to help him. "I know what you're going through. I've been there and done that. This is the course of it. This is what you do." I was able to comfort him.

What happens to you is not unique to you. Everybody has difficulties. And if we say, "Why me?" we miss what the Lord may want to be using the difficulty to teach us, to discipline us, to train us, to test us, to strengthen us, to prove us, in order that we may be able to help somebody else.

You Must Look Upward

Regardless of who you are or where you are, regardless of what's happening, the upward look is always open. Regardless of your circumstances, the upward look is always open. "I was among the captives." The captives numbered into the thousands. You can read Psalm 137 which talks about the people who were taken into captivity in Babylon, and they said:

By the rivers of Babylon, there we sat down, yea, we wept, when we remembered Zion. We hanged our harps upon the willows in the midst thereof. For there they that carried us away captive required of us a song; and they that wasted us required of us mirth, saying, Sing us one of the songs of Zion. — Psalm 137:1-3

And their response was:

How shall we sing the LORD'S song in a strange land? — Psalm 137:4

Here is a multitude of people looking around them. "We're captive. Our city is over 600 miles away. We'll never get back. We're wiped out. We're destroyed. Have pity!" And while they were looking around, Ezekiel looked up and saw visions of God.

About 40 years ago, I read a comic strip in the Sunday paper. I don't remember the name of the comic strip, but I remember each panel. I wish I'd clipped it and kept it. In the first panel was a picture of a chicken egg that is cracking open, and you can see the head of the little bitty coming out of the egg. In the second panel he is outside the egg, standing there shaking, and the fluid is flying off of him. In the third panel he is looking one direction—with fear, anxiety, and question marks in the little cloud—and he's totally confused. In the next panel, the fourth one, he's looking the opposite direction, and the cloud has even more of these asterisks and signs and question marks. In the fifth panel, he's looking right straight out at the reader, and the cloud covers the whole panel. He is just totally panic stricken. And in the last panel, he's trying to pull the egg back up around him and go back where he came from. What's wrong with the picture? He looked everywhere except up! That's the way we often react.

"I'm having a hard time. Hey, it's dark out there—forward, back, left, right—I can't see. I can't figure." Look up. It's always open. It's amazing that while other people were weeping and bemoaning, Ezekiel saw visions of God. Whatever else—verse 4 and following with all of this vision of the cherubim, the chariot, the turning, the one on the throne, the appearance on the throne, and the rainbow, again and again, "It was as... It was like... It was the appearance of"—whatever else it was, Ezekiel saw the glory of God.

You Need a Glimpse of God's Glory

This was the appearance of the likeness of the glory of the LORD. — Ezekiel 1:28

Let me submit to you, one of the greatest needs of the church in America—and we have many—but one of the greatest needs is that we get a fresh glimpse (for many people, maybe even the first glimpse) of the glory of God. What does glory of God mean? I am convinced it's one of the biggest words in all of language. The word *glory* has 13 different word forms in the Old Testament language that are translated *glory*. In the New Testament the primary word is *doxa*, and we use it when we sing "The Doxology." It basically means, "Praise God from whom all blessings." The word *glory* in the New Testament has 9 different word forms. I've read them all, and I've studied them all, and I have read what others have written about the glory of God; and, I tell you, it is beyond any one person's total comprehension.

For example, when the Bible speaks of the glory of God in the Old Testament in an outward sense, it speaks of size and immensity. Psalm 19 says that the heavens declare the glory of God. Wow, how's that for size! Go to where you stand at the edge of space, if you find that, and look out beyond you, and what do you see? You see more space. And as far as you can think, the heavens declare the glory of God.

It can be used to speak of size, and it can be used to speak of beauty. "Behold, the lilies of the field. They sow not, neither do they toil or spin, and yet I tell you that Solomon in all of his glory was not arrayed like one of these."

It's used not only for God and Christ and man, but it's even used for grass. The glory of the grass faded, withered. The flower passes away. It is whatever is the best of whatever—the best of the grass, the best of the flower, the best of something. Whatever it is, it's the best.

It has the idea of light, brilliance. That's what Ezekiel says here. The appearance was the likeness of the glory of the LORD. And he said it was the appearance of the brightness. The word is associated with light.

In the beginning God created the heaven and the earth. And the earth was without form, and void; and darkness was upon the face of the deep. And the Spirit of God moved upon the face of the waters. And God said, Let there be light: and there was light. — Genesis 1:1-3

Glory involves light, brilliant light, unfathomable light that just emanates. People say this light in Genesis 1:1-3 was the sun. No, it's not. The sun and moon didn't come until the fourth day of creation. This is a light that's unlike any other light.

Lastly, the word *glory* in the Old Testament, when used in an internal sense, can speak of purity. Psalm 45, a Messianic Psalm, says, "The king's daughter is all glorious within." It's amazing. It's such a big word. Ezekiel is saying, "I'm thinking. I've scratched my head, and I've tried to write it down. This was as that. This had the appearance of that. This was the likeness of that. It was as the appearance of the glory of God."

Whatever the glory of God is, it is the best of God. It is the most brilliant. It is the "omni" of God, "omni" meaning all. There's all-present, all-knowledgeable, all-powerful. It's that and everything else. It's all of His characteristics, His attributes, His faithfulness, His truth, His justice, His holiness, His love, His mercy, His wrath, His jealousy. Whatever you can say God is, it's all of that and more.

The problem with us is not that our God is too small, but that our concept of God is too small. What is your concept of God? To the average Christian, is God important? Well sure, He created everything, and He controls the heavens. Yes, but to the average person, He is not important. We trust our employer, and our social security, and our insurance, and our retirement, and all of that more than we trust the Lord. God's not important. I mean, we're supposed to go to church, but, "I want to go here instead." We're supposed to spend time in prayer, in Bible study, "But I'm too busy." Can you conceive it: "I'm too busy for God"? That's the unimportance of God. In Him we live and move and have our being, and yet to most people, God is not important.

As one man said to me, "Me and God have an agreement. I don't bother Him, and He doesn't bother me." That's a man who professed to be a believer. Whatever the glory of God is, it's something that we need to get a hold of and grasp. And if you ever do get a glimpse of the holiness, the greatness, the mightiness, the rightness, the glory of God, it will do to you what it did to Ezekiel. It will put you on your face.

You Need the Word of God to Come Expressly

The word of the LORD came expressly unto Ezekiel the priest, the son of Buzi, in the land of the Chaldeans by the river Chebar; and the hand of the LORD was there upon him. — Ezekiel 1:3 (emphasis added)

If you get some insight into the Person, the purity, and the holiness of God, the Word of the Lord becomes personal to you. Do you know what I'm talking about? It's not just a book. It becomes The Book. When you really get a glimpse of the glory of God, the Word of the Lord comes expressly to you, and God ministers to you.

I may read something that I have read literally hundreds of times, and—boom! Something new pops out. "I never thought of that. I never saw that. Wow! Thank God. There it is. How does that relate to this and to this?" The Word of the Lord comes expressly to you—Holy Bible book divine—thank God for His word. Peter said it: "He has given to us all things that pertain unto life and godliness." (2 Peter 1:3) He has already given it to us, and one of the things is His Word. The Word of the Lord comes expressly to you.

You Need the Hand of the Lord Upon You

The word of the LORD came expressly unto Ezekiel the priest, the son of Buzi, in the land of the Chaldeans by the river Chebar; and the hand of the LORD was there upon him. — Ezekiel 1:3 (emphasis added)

Do you have any idea what that is? Philip Voss was a friend of mine, a preacher in Hickory, North Carolina. He went to Israel with me on two occasions. Philip Voss got leukemia, the worst kind. Few survive that type of leukemia for more than 18 months. He lived 20. I was visiting him in the hospital. He was weak and emaciated, his body blue from his knees down, and spots of blue and purple all over. The leukemia was just killing him. He propped up in bed, pushed the button, raised himself a bit, and in a weak voice he said, "Let me tell you what happened to me this morning. It was about 4:00 this morning, and I was reading Revelation 1 where John saw the vision of the glory of God, and the vision of the resurrected Christ," and he said, "I got to the place where John fell on his face, and the Bible said, 'And He put His hand on my shoulder.'" And he said, "This morning I felt His hand on my shoulder."

I've never felt that physically, but I have felt the hand of God and the presence of the Lord in my life ministering to me to enable me to minister to somebody else. It's a hand of approval. It's a hand of acknowledgment. "You are My son. I approve of what you're doing, and I bless you and make you a blessing to others." Oh dear friend, if we could get a glimpse of the glory of God, the Word of the Lord would become expressly personal to us. The hand of the Lord would be upon us. You would humble yourself before God.

> *As the appearance of the bow that is in the cloud in the day of rain, so was the appearance of the brightness round about. This was the appearance of the likeness of the glory of the LORD. And when I saw it, I fell upon my face, and I heard a voice of one that spake. — Ezekiel 1:28*

You will humble yourself before the Lord. We think we are so great, don't we? We're so big in our own sight. Don't ask me who came up with these equations. I don't know where the scales are, but our earth weighs 6,600 quintillion tons. That's 6,600,000,000,000,000,000,000. Don't ask me who weighed it. Our sun could hold 1,300,000 of our earths within its surface.

One star in our galaxy would hold 99 million of our suns. There are about 100 billion stars in our galaxy. If you traveled at the speed of light, 186 thousand+ miles per second, if light carried you at that speed, you'd go around the world seven times in one second. But if you traveled at the speed of light from one end of our galaxy to the other end, it would take you about 100,000 years. Our galaxy is just one of an estimated 1 billion galaxies. Now how big do you feel?

Alas! and did my Savior bleed
And did my Sovereign die?
Would He devote that sacred head
For such a worm as I?

God help us! If we get a glimpse of God, it will put us on our face in humility. The Word of the Lord will come to you. The hand of the Lord will be upon you, and you will humble yourself before God.

And as we read in Ezekiel 1:28, **you will hear the voice of God.** I'm not saying that I hear God speak audibly, because I don't. But I do know what it's like to say, "The Lord impressed me. The Holy Spirit led me. God spoke to my heart." And if that doesn't resonate with you, if you don't relate to that, then you've never seen anything of the glory of God.

And he said unto me, Son of man, stand upon thy feet, and I will speak unto thee. — Ezekiel 2:1

He will stand you up on your feet. He'll stand you up. You don't stand up. If you humble yourself before God, He will exalt you at the right time. But if you try to elevate yourself, He will abase you and put you down. If you will fall on your face, the Lord will put you then on your feet.

You Need the Holy Spirit to Enter You

And the spirit entered into me when he spake unto me, and set me upon my feet, that I heard him that spake unto me. — Ezekiel 2:2 (emphasis added)

I was taught that in the Old Testament the Holy Spirit came upon a person for a purpose, for a certain period of time, but this says and means the Holy Spirit entered into him. You might argue, "Well, the Holy Spirit didn't enter into the believers until Jesus said, 'Receive the Holy Spirit.' And then later on the Day of Pentecost the power of the Holy Spirit came upon them." Yeah, but the Bible says the spirit of God entered into Ezekiel. Whatever else it means, it means that the Holy Spirit of God came in and upon Ezekiel in a way like he had never experienced it before.

You are Sent

And he said unto me, Son of man, I send thee to the children of Israel, to a rebellious nation that hath rebelled against me: they and their fathers have transgressed against me, even unto this very day. — Ezekiel 2:3

The sad truth is most Christians never lead anybody to Christ, and the big reason most people never lead anybody to Christ is because they never try. And the reason most people never try is that they've never had such an encounter with God. They don't see the glory of God. They don't see God as He is. They don't see themselves as they are. It is only after all of this that God said, "Now, Ezekiel, I'm sending you as My witness." It was only after Isaiah saw the Lord and saw himself that the Lord sent him. It was only after God had called Simon Peter, Andrew, James, John, Thomas, Bartholomew, and all of the disciples to be with Him, and then He would send them out.

Having a hard time? So is everybody. But God has a purpose for whatever is happening in your life. Greater is He that's in you than he that is in the world. Resist the devil and he'll flee from you. Be strong in the Lord and in the power of His might.

Rather than say, "Why has this happened?" focus on, "What do You want me to learn? How do You want to use this for Your own purposes, honor, and glory?" It would revolutionize your church, revolutionize your home, revolutionize your life if you would get alone and ask God to reveal more of Himself to you. If you get the vertical right, the horizontal will take care of itself. The clearer our vertical vision of God, the clearer we'll see the need of man. God help us to bring it from theory to reality. AMEN!

Chapter Five

Out of Bondage? Be Energized!
Ezra 9

Out of Bondage? Be Energized!
Ezra 9

Ezra was a scribe, who I believe wrote the books of Kings and Chronicles. He was a ready scribe. With the approval of the king, he came with about 50,000 people out of captivity back into the land of Israel. When they got into the land, everything had to be prepared and organized to set up a place of worship.

All these people had been contaminated with the captivity in Babylon for 70 years now. The vast majority of these people who come to the land of Israel were not born in Israel and taken into captivity. The vast majority of that first generation had died. These were people who were born in captivity and now had come into the land of Israel. They had to go through a ritual cleansing in the sixth chapter, setting aside and purifying the priests. Then we come to the ninth chapter, and we see several timeless truths.

Separation Under God is an Internal Matter

Separation under God is an internal matter, not external.

And the children of the captivity [the people of Israel] kept the passover upon the fourteenth day of the first month. For [or because] the priests and the Levites were purified together, all of them were pure, and killed the passover for all the children of the captivity, and for their brethren the priests, and for themselves. — Ezra 6:19

Now verse 20 says that the priests, the Levites, were purified together. But when we turn to chapter 9 and verse 1, some of the people came to Ezra and said, "The people, and the priests, and the Levites have not separated themselves from the people of the lands." They had been externally purified. They had gone through a ritual of washing, of bathing, of anointing with oil. Everything that was done to them was done in accordance to the law given by Moses, the Book of Leviticus, and everything was, as the Jews would say "kosher" or accepted; everything was fine. But when you come to the ninth chapter, they've not separated themselves. They have been separated externally, but not internally.

There are a lot of people who judge their separation under God based upon what they do not do. "If I don't do this or that, then I'm separated under God." When I was a kid growing up in a preacher's home, I thought separation was the only thing in the whole world that only had a negative side to it. My daddy was big on, "You can't do this, you can't do that, you can't go there, you can't have this." I thought separation had only one side, but I found out that there is a positive side.

Paul, a servant of Jesus Christ, called to be an apostle, separated unto the gospel of God. — Romans 1:1

Separation has two sides. It is not only what you are separated from but also what you are separated to. It's not only what you refuse to do, but also what you choose to do. It is positive. I was at a church in West Virginia years ago, when this man stood up and gave us his testimony. He shared about the many things that he did not do. He loved the Lord; he separated from the world. "I don't go to the movies. I don't do this. I don't dance." The man had such arthritis, he couldn't have danced if you had shot buck shot at his feet. He couldn't have seen the cards to gamble. He was in bad shape physically. There is an awful lot of stuff you don't do simply because you get old. You are not tempted to do what you can't do, right? There are a lot of people who judge their separation by what they do not do. No, you should judge it by what you do.

The priests were not separated socially in verse 1; they had not separated themselves from the people of the lands. They were not separated religiously. In verse 2, we read that they had intermarried with the pagan tribes around them. Separation is an internal matter. It is a matter of the heart.

Leadership Increases Responsibility

If you are in any position of leadership, your responsibility has increased. Now you may have no position of leadership, but you still have an influence. Everybody has an influence on somebody else, and you are to be setting a godly example.

When you are in a position of leadership, you have increased responsibility. In the latter part of verse 2, these people who were supposed to be the leaders, the holy seed, had "mingled themselves with the people of those lands, the hand of the princes and rulers had been chief in this trespass." Instead of the leaders leading in the way of godliness, they were the leaders in the intermingling and the intermarrying. A position of leadership increases responsibility. James talks about that in the book

My brethren, be not many masters, knowing that we shall receive the greater condemnation. — James 3:1

I live with very little fear. I am not a fearful person. But I am afraid of things that sting, not because I am afraid of the creature necessarily. I'm afraid of the results of being stung because I know I will get sick and have to go to a hospital if I get a lot of bee or wasp stings. So I fear them. I respect those fellows, but I'm not afraid of "stuff." I'm not fearful by nature, but there are certain things that I fear.

Another thing that I fear is the judgment seat of Christ. I know in our culture we've about turned it into a jubilee, but I don't particularly look forward to standing before the Lord in judgment and giving an account for every idle word. I don't enjoy the thought of giving account for everything I've done, good and bad, but I'll have to do that. A position of leadership increases your responsibility.

It's Okay to Be Emotional about the Right Things

You can tell a lot about a person by the things that excite him. Recently I saw a church sign that read, "Your character will be revealed by what makes you mad, sad, or glad." What moves you? It is okay to be emotional about the right things. When the report came to Ezra that these people who are supposed to be leaders in godliness and righteousness were actually leaders in intermarrying, committing abominations, and worshipping of idols, look what it did to Ezra in verse 3: "And when I heard this thing, I rent my garment." This is a Jewish oriental sign of grief. But Ezra goes even beyond the normal expression of grief and tears his mantle, too.

What is a mantle? Not the one over the fireplace. A mantle is a prayer shawl. They first began using them during the Babylonian captivity. Even today you see the men at the western wall in Jerusalem going to pray and placing a prayer shawl over their head. The mantle is their tabernacle that shuts out the world, and they wear that prayer shawl over their head to help focus and concentrate. It is just tradition now, but when you are a captive in Babylon and your temple, 700 or 800 miles away, has been destroyed, that little prayer shawl would remind you of the covering of God's blessing and promises. So you put on that prayer shawl. Ezra tore that!

I have seen a few dirty Jews that look like they haven't had a bath in a month. I've seen dirty clothes, dirty shoes, dirty shirts, but I have never ever seen a dirty prayer shawl. Never. And certainly not one that was torn. His clothes may be torn, but his prayer shawl will be clean. But Ezra tore his prayer shawl. This man is beside himself with grief. He is astonished, the Bible says.

And when I heard this thing, I rent my garment and my mantle, and plucked off the hair of my head and of my beard, and sat down astonied. Then were assembled unto me every one that trembled at the words of the God of Israel, because of the transgression of those that had been carried away; and I sat astonied until the evening sacrifice. — Ezra 9:3-4

He's lost, and he sat there. "And I sat there until 3:00 in the afternoon." The morning sacrifice is at 9:00. The evening sacrifice is at 3:00 because the day begins at sundown. That's the evening sacrifice. Jesus was put on the cross at the time of the morning sacrifice and died at the time of the evening sacrifice at 3:00 in the afternoon. Ezra said, "I sat there all day." This man has really lost it.

Then there came a group of people—thank God for these folks—they came and trembled at the words of the Lord God of Israel. They trembled at the word because of the transgression of those being carried away. Then, verse 5:

And at the evening sacrifice I arose up from my heaviness; [my affliction] and having rent my garment and my mantle, I fell upon my knees. — Ezra 9:5

Christians know about prayer on our knees, but Jews do not normally kneel. Solomon did when he dedicated the temple, Ezra did here, but that is the exception. Generally, they are either standing or lying flat on their face. "I can't cover my head and I spread out my hands, and I prayed, and said, 'God, I'm ashamed and I blush to lift up my face to You.'" Would you say he is emotional? Yeah, he is having a meltdown, whatever terminology you want to use. It is okay to be emotional if it is about the right things. We sing, "Weep o'er the erring one, lift up the fallen. Tell them of Jesus, the mighty to save. Rescue the perishing, care for the dying."

Have you ever wept over an erring one? Have you ever lifted up the fallen? If you have a member of your church who is faithful and then doesn't come anymore, have you ever wept over such a one? Have you ever been broken up because of anybody's sin? Your sin? Anybody else's sin? How long since you've wept over anything besides a movie or a television program? Isn't it amazing that we are so unemotional about things that ought to evoke emotions?

Innocent People are Affected by the Sins of Others

And said, O my God, I am ashamed and blush to lift up my face to thee, my God: for our iniquities are increased over our head, and our trespass is grown up unto the heavens. Since the days of our fathers have we been in a great trespass unto this day; and for our iniquities have we, our kings, and our priests, been delivered into the hand of the kings of the lands, to the sword, to captivity, and to a spoil, and to confusion of face, as it is this day. — Ezra 9:6-7

That is such a phrase, "confusion of face." We are God's people, but we don't look like it. I think one of the striking examples of this was Jonah, when he was called out of sleep onto the deck during that hurricane, and the sailors asked him, "Who are you? Where are you from?" This is a man that ran from God and went to sleep in the sides of the ship, and when they began to identify who he was, "Maybe you are the one who has caused this storm to come," Jonah said, "I am a Hebrew, and I fear the Lord God." What? You are Hebrew all right, but you don't fear the Lord God or you would have obeyed Him. Ezra says, "It is confusion of face." We are not what we appear to be. We are God's people, but for centuries we've not lived like God's people.

Daniel, Shadrach, Meshach, and Abednego went into the captivity in Babylon. Ezekiel also went into the captivity in Babylon. He was a priest in Jerusalem—loyal, serving God, and yet he went into captivity. Do you think those guys did anything that deserved being taken captive? No. The three Hebrew friends of Daniel, Daniel himself, Ezekiel, others, godly people—and yet when the nation had sinned so much that God sent judgment, these innocent were taken into captivity as well.

You may think "if I'm hurting anybody, I'm only hurting myself." No, you aren't, friend. You are hurting the whole Body of Christ when you sin. A lot of people, innocent people, have to suffer because of the sins of other people. If we would remember the far-reaching effects of sin—like ripples on a water when you throw a pebble into the pond and the ripples keep going—if we could see the far-reaching effect of our sin, it might slow us down and prevent some of the sinning.

Grace Extended Must Be Appropriated

And now for a little space [a little moment, a little time] grace hath been shewed from the Lord our God, to leave us a remnant to escape, and to give us a nail [a place of surety] in his holy place, that our God may lighten our eyes, [illuminate our minds] and give us a little reviving in our bondage.
— Ezra 9:8

Grace has been extended. Dear friend, when grace is extended, grace must be appropriated. The world is wicked, full of false imaginations, and a man's heart is only wicked continually. God said, "I will destroy man from off the face of the earth which I've created," but Noah found grace in the eyes of the Lord. He doesn't say, "In 120 days I'm going to destroy the world." He said 120 years. That is plenty of grace, isn't it? Grace is extended, but they didn't repent. So judgment came.

The people of Sodom and Gomorrah and the cities of the plain had heavenly angels who came and would have brought out anybody and everybody who wanted to escape the judgment. Dear friend, that is grace. But when the grace was spurned, the judgment came, and the cities were destroyed.

When Jonah finally got right with God, and came into Nineveh and began to preach, he didn't preach 40 minutes, "Nineveh will be overthrown." He preached 40 days. That is grace. The most amazing thing happened. Jonah 3 says, "The people of Nineveh believed God." Isn't that refreshing? They proclaimed a fast, and the king (who isn't even named) said, "Everybody turn from the violence that is your own hand and call upon God. Who shall say? Maybe God will turn and not do unto us the thing that He said He would do." And the Bible says:

*And God saw their works, that they turned from their evil
way; and God repented of the evil, that he had said that he
would do unto them; and he did it not. — Jonah 3:10*

Grace, when it is extended, must be appropriated, must be
received. How many opportunities to be saved does God owe
you? None! Not one. How many opportunities have you had?
God's Spirit does not always strive with people, and your heart
becomes so hard you can't hear the voice of the Lord calling
you to come to repentance.

Nobody will be in Heaven against their will. Grace, favor—
God has favored us. He has preserved a remnant of us, and He
is giving us this opportunity to come. He is going to illumine
our minds, lighten our minds, give us a little reviving in the
bondage. Grace extended must be appropriated.

God's Mercy is More than We Deserve, and His Wrath Less than We Deserve

*For we were bondmen; yet our God hath not forsaken us
in our bondage, but hath extended mercy unto us in the
sight of the kings of Persia, to give us a reviving, to set up
the house of our God, and to repair the desolations thereof,
and to give us a wall in Judah and in Jerusalem. — Ezra 9:9*

We were in bondage. We were not forsaken. We were extended mercy. He has given us a reviving, to sit up, to repair,
to build a wall and a defense. God has not treated us as we
deserve.

The story is told of a lady who posed for a painting, day after
day after day. She was a very vain lady yet not too pretty, but
the artist tried his best. When he finally finished and showed it
to her, he said, "Your thoughts, Madame?" She said, "It doesn't
do me justice." He answered, "Madame, you don't need justice. You need mercy." And so with us all. If we got justice,
where would we be? Thank God! Mercy is not getting what we
deserve! My daddy would get ready to whip me, and I'd cry,
"Have mercy! Have mercy!" not "give me what I deserve." That

is mercy, not getting what you deserve. Grace is getting what you don't deserve.

Christianity is Not Just Saying, but Doing
And now, O our God, what shall we say after this? — *Ezra 9:10*

You have to read into the next chapter to find out about Shecaniah. You have probably never heard his name. His name means "he dwells with God." He is not a governor or a leader, but he is standing there when Ezra, who is the leader, doesn't know what to do: "What are we going to do? What are we going to do? What can we say more? What do we do?" And from the crowd, Shecaniah opens his mouth and says, "I know what we can do." What? "We can repent. We can get right!"

That's exactly what to do. Every preacher, every pastor needs members of his church whose names are Shecaniah, who encourage us to get right.

Though this happened 400 to 500 years before our Lord, roughly 2,500 years ago, it is just as applicable today as it was the day it was said. We were bondmen. We were in sin. We deserve justice, but we were granted mercy. And God brought us out of our bondage, out of a horrible pit, put our feet on a rock, a solid rock! He gave us a song in our hearts. And we have responsibilities as saved people. God help us not to goof it up, to waste our time or our talents. AMEN!

Chapter Six

Christ in the Storms
Mark 4, 6

Christf in the Storms
Mark 4:35-41, Mark 6:45-52

Much of the ministry of Jesus was centered in the area of Galilee. It is a section of the country the center of which, of course, is the lake or the Sea of Galilee. It is about seven miles at its widest point and about 14 miles long, teardrop-shaped. Of all of the places that I've ever been—not just in Israel, and Jordan, and Egypt, but anywhere I've ever been for that matter —Galilee is my favorite place in all the earth.

There is a tranquility and a peace about it. In March, the hillsides are green with grass and ablaze with color of mustard yellow and red poppies, white flowers, blue flowers, flowers of all colors. You've never seen a sunrise until you've see the sun rise over the hills of the Golan Heights and bounce off the water on the Sea of Galilee. Most of the ministry of Jesus was in that area.

The city of Capernaum is now in ruins, much of it excavated all the way down to the base of the synagogue that was there in the time of Christ. The house of Simon the fisherman and apostle, as well as much of the city, has been excavated until there is no city of Capernaum now. It was the only city of any size around the Lake of Galilee, and it is a lovely spot.

The surface of the water in the Sea of Galilee is over 600 feet below sea level. Off to the west, where the winds come in, there is a pass that comes all the way from the Mediterranean Sea by Mount Carmel at Haifa. The wind comes all across the Sharon Plain, the Valley of Megiddo, around Nazareth at over 1,400 feet above sea level, and then down a pass from the mountains of Nazareth down to that lake that is 600 feet below sea level. That wind can come rushing in and in five minutes time can transform from absolute calm to tremendous waves that would sink a boat. Storms come up suddenly and often in the dark of night.

In my life it seems that storms come at the worst possible time, but is there ever a good time for trouble? It seems that the storms often arrive in the night. The storms come up suddenly.

We are going through life, sailing. The sea is calm, everything is under control, the engines are running, we are on course, everything is on schedule. And suddenly, from nowhere, in the middle of the dark, here comes the wind and the storm. It always hits us, and we're never ready. Isn't that amazing? We know they'll come, we know they'll come suddenly, and yet we're not ready for them.

He is Watching

In Mark 4, Jesus is in the boat. But the presence of Christ in the boat does not prevent the storms from coming. Even though He is in the boat, the storms can come. In Mark 4 and Mark 6, the disciples are in the boat at His instruction; they are not running from Him. In one instance He is with them, and the second instance He sent them, constrained them, commanded them to get in the boat and go to the other side. In both instances they are doing what He told them to do, yet the storms came.

The presence of Christ in your life does not mean that you won't have storms. At salvation, some of your problems will be solved. The eternal problems of heaven and hell, that'll be solved, but not everyday problems. In fact, when you give your life to Christ, you're going to have problems you never had before because you've become a child of God, the object of the hatred of the devil. We always are amazed that the world gives us a hard time. A young boy said to me a couple of days ago, "How is the world treating you?" and I responded, "The world hates me." He had no concept of what I was talking about, and he was a believer. Yet, the presence of Christ in the boat does not mean you will avoid the storms.

In the fourth chapter, the disciples see Him. He is in the boat, and they can see Him. In the sixth chapter, they can't see Him. He is on land, and it is dark in the fourth watch of the night. He is out of their sight; they don't see Him. There are times in my Christian experience, when I am closer to Him than at other times. There are times when I can see His leading more clearly than at other times. There are times when frankly it is not difficult. Then there are other times when it is very difficult.

In Mark 4, Jesus is asleep; in Mark 6, Jesus is awake. Isn't that odd? In the fourth chapter, when He was so near them, He was asleep. In the sixth chapter, when He was so far from them, He was awake. And they're saying, "Where is He?" All the while in the middle of the night in a storm at least five miles away from them, catch this now, the Bible said, "And He saw them toiling in rowing." Whether I can see Him or not. Whether He is in the boat or not. Whether He is so close that I can say, "There He is!" or He is so far away that I cry out, "Where is He?" Whether He is near us, or far from us, whether we think He is asleep and unconscious to our danger, unconscious to our peril, unconscious to our need, He is watching. He sees, and He knows.

He is Sufficient

In the fourth chapter, they wake Him up, and He speaks to the wind, and to the sea. To the one, he says to the wind, "Peace," and it stops. To the second, he says to, "Be still," and it is calm. In the sixth chapter, He speaks to the disciples. He was walking toward them on the water in the wind and the waves, and He speaks to them. He walked up to them and says, "Be of good cheer." It literally means, "Be of good comfort." "It is I. Be not afraid."

In some of the storms, in some of the experiences, He will minister to us this way. Whatever is needed, He will miraculously change the situation, and give us calmness as a result. I mean, it is understandable to be afraid when you are in the middle of the lake that is 150 feet deep, and you're three and a half miles from shore. When you've exhausted yourself from rowing against the wind and the waves, and the boat is full of water, it is understandable to be fearful. In that situation, He spoke to the wind and to the waves, and there is a calm. So He doesn't need to say anything to them, the danger has passed.

In the second situation, when He is outside the boat and coming towards them, He says, "Be of good comfort. It is I. Be not afraid." Now wait a minute, the waves are still piling up and getting into the boat, the wind is still boisterous, but He said, "Be of great comfort. It is I. Be not afraid." And other times, He will minister to us by saying, "Even though the storm is raging, here I am. Be of good comfort. It is I. Be not afraid."

Wouldn't it have been easier for Him to just all at once appear in the boat? You know He is on the mountain, and if He can walk on the water, surely He can just transport Himself from the mountain to the middle of the boat and say the same thing again. "Peace, be still." Why didn't He do it that way? Instead, He comes toward them on the water. It takes time to come down from the mountain and walk on the water to where they are. We're talking three and a half miles of walking on water, not counting walking on land. That takes a while. Wouldn't it have been simpler just to zap Himself right down into the middle of the boat? That's the way we want it. They would have recognized Him had He done it that way, but here He does it completely differently, walking toward them, and they don't recognize Him. I think sometimes we miss Him when He comes to minister to us because He does it in such strange ways.

Whether you recognized Him because He is so close to you in the boat, or whether you don't recognize Him because you left Him on the mountain and it's dark and stormy, and suddenly here comes something on the water that you think is a ghost. He is coming to minister, to meet your needs. Blessed be His name.

In Chapter 4, He stands up. In Chapter 6, He gets in the boat. Everything is different, isn't it? In Chapter 4, it was a big dark storm so severe the people thought they were going to drown. But one thing above all things that is consistent whether it is Chapter 4 or Chapter 6 is that He is sufficient. Whether you see Him, or whether you don't. Whether you recognize Him or whether you don't. Whether He is near you or whether He is on the mountain—He is sufficient. Whether He needs to stand up, or whether He needs to get in the boat—He is sufficient. Whether it is calm water or stormy water—He is sufficient. Whether it is sunshine or midnight—He is sufficient. Whatever the situation—He is sufficient for whatever the problem.

He is in Control

Now how do I react to all of that? I think, "I am in this storm, in the will of God." Now hear that. I am in the difficult situation in the will of God. Being in the will of God doesn't exempt you from storms, and being in a storm doesn't automatically mean you are out of the will of God.

There was a fellow by the name of Job, who got in a storm because he was in the will of God. If I am in the will of God, I can say, "I am in this difficult situation in the will of God." That gives me such assurance, and such security. You know Satan is not going to do anything to you, or to me, but what God permits. Satan is the one who goes to and fro, not the Lord. The Lord doesn't go to and fro; He is already everywhere. Satan comes before God and asks permission to afflict Job, and God sets the borders of how far it can go. God is in control. If I am in the will of God, then the storm is also in the will of God. Then I can say, "Since I am in the will of God, and in the storm, then I will be preserved in the storm."

It's not because of my rowing, not because of my toiling through the night, not because of my expertise as a sailor, not because of the boat or the condition of the boat. If I am in the will of God, I am in the storm in the will of God, and I have been preserved in the storm because of the Christ who ministers to me. Then I can say, "I'll survive the storm." You may think you're not going to make it, but you're going to make it.

He that hath begun a good work in you will perform it until the day of Jesus Christ. — Phil. 1:6

Finally, the Lord said, "Go to the other side." He didn't say, "Go out in the middle of the lake and drown." He said, "We're going to the other side." So whether it is sunshine and a steady breeze, or whether it is midnight and storms, ultimately, some golden daybreak Jesus will come. And I'll sail this sea no more. I'll land safe on the other side. Hallelujah!

I tell you, He is a sufficient Christ. So what are you going to do? Are you going to row all night long? Are you going to exhaust yourself? Or are you going to say, whether He is in the boat, or whether He is walking on the water, "Here He is. I'll let Him minister to me, with the assurance that I am in the will God in the storm. He will preserve me in the storm. I will survive the storm, and I will arrive safely on the other side." Why don't we just quit the worrying and the rowing? Why don't we look and realize that the boat leaks horribly anyhow? Our sufficiency is not in the oars or in the boat or in the sails; our sufficiency is in the Savior. If you are in the storm in the will of God, you'll survive the storm and come safely to shore. AMEN!

Chapter Seven

Spirit Filled? Expect This!
Luke 4

Spirit Filled? Expect This!
Luke 4

And be not drunk with wine, wherein is excess; but be filled with the Spirit. – Ephesians 5:18

None of us has ever seen a man filled with wine. If you were to cut him open, he has lungs, liver, stomach, spleen and all kinds of stuff in him. But what you have seen is a person controlled by wine. Similarly, to be filled with the Spirit is to be controlled by the Spirit.

Every believer possesses the Spirit, "for by one Spirit are we all baptized into one body." When we are saved, we receive the earnest of the Spirit, the sealing of the Spirit, yet we are still told to be filled with the Spirit. In the original language, this is called a middle voice. It means that the responsibility rests upon us. My own translation of this verse says, "Be not drunk [controlled] with wine which leads to debauchery, but be ye (of yourselves) continually being filled [controlled] by the Holy Spirit."

How does this happen? What does it mean to be filled with the Spirit? It seems logical to me, that if I want to learn what to expect when I'm filled with the Spirit, I should go back to the source; I should look at Christ.

And Jesus being full of the Holy Ghost returned from Jordan, and was led by the Spirit into the wilderness. – Luke 4:1

And Jesus returned in the power of the Spirit into Galilee. – Luke 4:14

The Spirit of the Lord is upon me. – Luke 4:18

In verse 1, Christ is "full of the Holy Ghost" and "led by the spirit." In verse 14, Jesus "returned in the power of the Spirit." And, in verse 18, "the Spirit of the Lord was upon Christ." Other references in Matthew's account and Mark's account say that He was "driven by the Spirit." As we look at these verses about the Holy Spirit in the life of Christ, we see that being filled with the Holy Spirit means being led and directed by the Spirit.

Being full of the Spirit does not mean that you will have immediate success in your life. Being filled and controlled of the Spirit does not mean that you will have immediate success in your ministry, in your job, or whatever it is that God has for you to do.

It doesn't mean that at all. After Jesus was baptized and the Spirit of God was sent in the form of a dove, rather than begin to preach that the Kingdom of Heaven is at hand, Christ disappeared for forty days. He was led and driven by the Spirit into the wilderness to be tempted of the devil. If Christ, filled with the Holy Spirit, did not experience immediate success, you can't expect immediate success.

Do you want to be filled with the Spirit? Do you want to be filled and controlled by the experience of God? You can't expect immediate success, but there are a few things you can expect.

Expect to Wait

When you are filled with the Holy Spirit, you can expect to wait. It runs that way throughout the Word of God. I'll give you two examples. One is from the Old Testament, the story of the prophet Elijah. He walked out of the mountains of Gilead into the palace and the presence of a pagan King. He said, "It isn't going to rain any more until I say so." Then, he walked out ,knowing that he had spoken the truth.

But instead of God letting him go out to be a prophet—and God knows the land needed one—God put Elijah by a brook and fed him with what a dirty, unclean, non-kosher bird brought him to eat. Here's a young prophet raring to go, eager to preach, and for three years God didn't let him preach at all.

Elijah, filled with the Spirit, was expected to wait.

We see an example of this in the life of a New Testament counterpart, Paul, as well. After Paul was saved on the road to Damascus, he immediately began to testify that Jesus was the Messiah. But not for long. Soon God sent him into the Arabian Desert for a long time—alone. Paul, filled with the Spirit, was expected to wait. When you are filled with the Spirit of God, don't expect immediate service or immediate success; expect to wait.

Expect to be Tested

"Oh, if I just get filled with the Spirit of God, I'm going to sail above the problems. I'm not going to be under the circumstances. Everything is going to be wonderful and rosy." Not so. Jesus was led and driven by the Spirit into the wilderness—not woods, trees, rocks, and creeks, but barren land. Forty days Jesus was there in the wilderness. At the end of the forty days, then came that test. "Since you are the Son of God, do this. Since you are the Bread of Life, command that rock to be bread." You, too, can expect to be tested.

"Well, I'm never tested by the devil," you might say. Then you aren't doing anything in the battle. The truth of the matter is that the reason Satan doesn't bother a lot of believers is that he's already neutralized them. They aren't a factor in the battle, and they are not causing him any problem.

Are you in the battle? Does the devil even know who you are? In the New Testament, there were some young prophets who wanted to cast demons out of a fellow. The demons cried out, "Jesus we know, and Paul we know, but who are you?" The demons didn't know them. Instead of the young prophets driving the devils out, the devils drove them out of the house. Are you a factor in the battle? The Lord knows who you are, but does the devil? If so, then you can expect to be tested.

This was also true in the life of Paul. Cast down but not destroyed, always bearing about in the body the dying of the Lord Jesus Christ. Following Christ, living in the power of the Holy Spirit—it's not easy. You can expect to be tested, and you can expect to wait.

Expect to be Strengthened

After Jesus was tested in the wilderness, the Gospels of Matthew and Mark both say of Jesus experience, "And the angels came and ministered unto him." When the testing comes, you can expect to be strengthened by the Lord, too.

We see an example of this in the life of Paul. Paul knew what it meant to be tested.

Go thy way: for [Paul] he is a chosen vessel unto me, to bear my name before the Gentiles, and kings, and the children of Israel: For I will shew him how great things he must suffer for my name's sake. – Acts 9:15-16

Paul himself said, "In me first a pattern of my suffering should to all them that believe. No man stood by me, but the Lord stood by me." In his testing, Paul was strengthened by the Lord.

You can expect to be strengthened with the help of the Lord. You have to call on it, you have to ask for it, you have to believe it, and you have to rest in it. You can expect yourself to be stronger because of the test. It makes you stronger. If you have it easy, you get flabby—spiritually flabby. Your faith gets weak. It's the severity of the test that makes you stronger.

"Well, Jesus was weak at the end of the forty days," you might say. But I suggest to you that Jesus was stronger at the end of forty days than He was at the beginning of it, for He comes to the end of His own strength, and is dependent upon the strength of the Lord.

Expect to Battle the Flesh

And when the devil had ended all the temptation, he departed from him for a season. And Jesus returned in the power of the Spirit into Galilee. — Luke 4:13-14

The devil departed. What a victory! The devil had thrown tests and temptations at Him that were physical. "Command the stones to be made bread." The tests and temptations were also emotional and spiritual. "I'll give you all the Kingdoms of the World right now if you'll bow down." Jesus conquered him every time by the Word of God. What a victory!

Do you know that the greatest battle generally comes after the victory? Think of Elijah on Mt. Carmel against 850 false prophets. He gains the victory, then flees from Jezebel, goes down to hide in the wilderness, and prays to die. The victory is good, but after the victory the temptation is for the flesh to take over.

Our Scripture does not say, "Jesus returned unto Galilee." It says, "He returned in the power of the Spirit into Galilee." It's not by accident that the Holy Spirit adds that phrase. You can expect to be continually battling the human flesh. That's the human tendency.

We all battle the flesh. Whether it's 17-year-old, or 87-year old flesh, flesh is flesh. The devil knows your weak point, though the weak point at one stage in your life may not be the weak point at another stage in your life. You could not tempt David with a Bathsheba when he was an old man, but he surely was tempted when he was a younger man. When he was an older man, he fell victim to pride in numbering the soldiers. His tendency then was to depend on the 1,580,000 under him rather than the one God who is over him. We always battle the flesh.

For I know that in me (in my flesh), dwelleth no good thing. — *Romans 7:18*

O wretched man that I am! who shall deliver me from the body of this death? — *Romans 7:24*

This is a faithful saying, and worthy of all acceptation, that Christ Jesus came into the world to save sinners; of whom I am chief. — *1 Timothy 1:15*

We say *am* and think *was*. But at the beginning of his ministry, Paul said, "I am the least of the apostles." At the middle of his ministry, he said, "I am less than the least." At the end of his ministry, he said, "I am the chief of sinners." It's not a new young preacher who says, "I am chief." It's the old saint, as Paul the aged calls himself, who says, "I am chief of sinners."

Expect to be Faithful

And he came to Nazareth, where he had been brought up: and, as his custom was, he went into the synagogue on the sabbath day, and stood up for to read. — Luke 4:16

Now, whether his custom was to go up and read every Sabbath, I don't know. I suspect not, but I know that his custom was to be faithful to worship. I go to Sunday morning service and Sunday night and Wednesday night. I go to witness to people. Why? I'm supposed to. Not because I'm a super saint, but because I'm supposed to. God's not going to use a lazy person. "Well, I'm filled with the Spirit." Yes, but you need to be in fellowship with God's people. You need to be faithful in the house of the Lord, and thank God you are here.

Expect to Serve

The Spirit of the Lord is upon me, because he hath anointed me to preach the gospel to the poor; he hath sent me to heal the brokenhearted, to preach deliverance to the captives, and recovering of sight to the blind, to set at liberty them that are bruised, To preach the acceptable year of the Lord. — Luke 4:18-19

In those phrases, we see a combination of what we are and what we are to do. I am to preach, to heal, and to announce deliverance, to give sight to the blind and to set at liberty them that are bruised, to announce the acceptable year of the Lord. The idea is, if you are genuinely controlled by the Spirit, your motivation will be to serve rather than to be served. Ask yourself, "Would I rather serve or be served?" Think about it. Would you rather serve or be served?

The greatest blessing that you can receive is the blessing of being a blessing. Jesus said, "I'm sent to preach the Gospel." "I'm sent to set at liberty the captive." "I'm sent to do this…"

Don't you think He enjoyed that? Don't you think it was a blessing to Him?

Expect Opposition and Success

If we had the time to read the rest of the chapter, you would read that while some people thoroughly enjoyed the ministry of our Lord—some people were healed, and some people were blessed—others opposed Him and got all bent out of shape. You want to be spirit-filled? Expect opposition, but at the same time expect success.

And all they in the synagogue, when they heard these things, were filled with wrath, And rose up, and thrust him out of the city, and led him unto the brow of the hill (Nazareth) whereon their city was built, that they might cast him down headlong. — Luke 4:28-29

"A great and effectual door is opening unto me," Paul said, "and there are many adversaries." The victory is only sweeter as the battle is harder. If you want victory, the greater victory comes from the greater battle. What I'm telling you is this, I believe this with all my heart: most people who say, "I want to be filled with the Spirit," don't want to be filled with the Spirit. They want the feeling of the Spirit. But there's a vast difference between the feeling and the filling. You want the filling of the Spirit. Let me suggest that you do the following:

- Ask God to bring to your mind every sin and confess it.
- Ask God to fill you and to control you.
- Accept it by faith.

How did you get saved? Did you get saved by faith or by feeling? You got the feeling afterwards, right? Thank God for the feeling, but you weren't saved by feeling, you were saved by faith. How do you have the filling, the controlling of the Spirit? Pray, "Lord, cleanse me from every sin, and that one too. Thank you for bringing that one to mind. God, forgive me for that. Make me a clean vessel. Now Lord, fill me, control me. Just as I accepted You as my Savior by faith, I accept the filling of the Spirit by faith, and I want to live controlled by the Spirit of God." AMEN!

Chapter Eight

What God Desires From Us
Luke 10, John 10, 12

What God Desires From Us
Luke 10, John 10, 12

Now it came to pass, as they went, that he entered into a certain village: and a certain woman named Martha received him into her house. And she had a sister called Mary, which also sat at Jesus' feet, and heard his word. — Luke 10:38

Martha means mistress, overseer, the lady, hospitable, focused, work-oriented, a worrier, in fact. She's like a lot of people I know that, if they don't have anything to worry about, they worry about the fact that they've forgotten something to worry about. I know people like that.

But Martha is in charge. The Bible says it's her house. That's unusual. Houses were owned by men. I can only guess, but I suspect that Martha is the eldest, that her husband is dead, and that he owned the house. There's no mention of children, no mention of marriage. I don't know whether we're talking about a widow, an old maid, and a bachelor. I don't know. But it's rare and odd that the woman owns the house. Yet, it's definitely her house. She's the overseer.

There are nine different women in the New Testament named Mary. It took me a good while to find the meaning, because many people have different ideas. It's a very old name. Some students and scholars had said that Mary means bitter, and when I read that, I thought that doesn't sound like Mary. She's sweetness and light, not bitter. I went back and checked in the Hebrew language, and the root of the word is mara, where Naomi came back into Bethlehem and said, "Don't call me Naomi, which means pleasant. Call me Mara which means bitter, because the Lord has dealt very bitterly with me." (Ruth 1:20) This didn't sound right.

Then I learned that the name Miriam, the Hebrew word for Mary, the New Testament Greek word, and then Latin, and then Italian, and then English Mary, Maria, comes from that word mara. I thought, "This can't be right." I did a little bit more digging and voilà, it's an Egyptian word. It's older than Genesis so far as we don't read the word Mary or Miriam, the Old Testament word, until we meet Miriam who is the sister of Moses in the book of Exodus. Her name Miriam in the Egyptian language was "Mry," and it means beloved. That seems better. Mary is the beloved.

Lazarus's real name was Elazarus. The servant of Abraham was Eliazar in the Hebrew, transferred into the New Testament. When Jerome translated from the Old Testament from Hebrew into Latin in the late 300's he dropped the 'E' which is not spoken anyhow, and it became not Elazarus, but Lazarus. It's significant because the word Elazarus means "God has helped," or "he whom God helps," as the servant of Abraham. But Lazarus means "without help." Everybody is either a Lazarus or an Elazarus. You are either without help, or if you're saved, it's because God has helped or delivered you. Amen!

From the lives of these three people—Martha, Mary, and Lazarus—we will look at some things that God desires for us.

But Martha was cumbered about much serving, and came to him, and said, Lord, dost thou not care that my sister hath left me to serve alone? bid her therefore that she help me. And Jesus answered and said unto her, Martha, Martha, thou art careful and troubled about many things: But one thing is needful: and Mary hath chosen that good part, which shall not be taken away from her. — Luke 10:40-42

The relationship between Jesus and these three—Martha, Mary, and Lazarus—was unique. Lazarus is not one of the twelve. He lives with Martha. It's just over the hill from the Mount of Olives, just a little less than two miles from the Temple Mount in Jerusalem, a Sabbath's Day journey. When Jesus came to Jerusalem, which was not often, He evidently stayed at their home. When He'd come at a feast day, like this Passover just before He will be crucified, the city would be full of people. There are no available rooms in the house. You would stay in homes, and Jesus would go to their house and stay with them. You don't have to be one of the twelve to be in good, close relationship with Jesus. From these three people and three separate instances, I want to draw out for you six things that the Lord would desire of us.

Your Talent

The Lord wants your talent. The Lord wants your ability. That's the first thing He wants. In Luke 10, when Jesus arrives at their house, Martha is serving. She's an overseer. She's a mistress. She's in charge, and she's hospitable. Thank God for people who have a gift of hospitality. My wife has that. She's a great hostess and hospitable. That's why I weigh 210 pounds. She's a southern woman. If you love it, feed it, and she's just that way.

But Martha is upset. She said, "Tell my sister to come and help me. There's one of You and twelve others with You. That's 13 people. I've got to feed You, 13, plus Lazarus, Mary, and myself, and she's not helping me." It would have seemed logical that Mary should be helping her. Yet, the Lord chided Martha, "You are anxious and troubled about many things." The Lord said to her, "You are anxious and troubled. You're frustrated. You have anxiety." Isn't that a terrible way to serve Jesus? It's not that He was upbraiding her because of what she was doing, serving instead of sitting and listening to Him teach as Mary was doing. He upbraids her because of her attitude. It's good to have talent and use it for what God has given you. But Martha is envious that Mary is listening: "I want to be listening; but He's in my house, and I'm obligated to feed them." She's doing the logical thing to do. When He upbraids her it's not because she's serving, she's cooking, and she's preparing. It's because of the attitude.

You can be in the service of God and have a lousy attitude, and lose all of the reward and all of the joy of serving. The Lord wants your talent, but He wants you to do it with a cheerful heart.

Several years ago, I wrote these words:

- *Why must man's innate potential stay bound in chains that yet grant ease,*
- *And mediocrity seem so normal, that man from true achievement flees?*
- *Were there one of us who nurtured all those gifts he had received,*
- *The rest of us would brand him foolish and feel relieved.*

It's true. We sing, "Give of your best to the Master. Give of the strength of your youth." And if the guy gets up with his guitar and his wife standing there, and he's got to tune it up. I wonder, why didn't he tune it up before church? "Pray for us. We haven't had time to practice," he says. And I just have to bite my lip to keep from saying that if you haven't had time to practice, I don't have time to listen to you sing. If you're going to do it for the Lord, give it your best. The Lord wants your talent, but He wants the best that you have, not the leftovers. Going to different churches week after week, more than a few times I've gotten up and left a Sunday School class to think over my sermon and pray, because the guy got up and said, "I haven't had time to study, so we'll just go through it together." Well, if he doesn't have time to study, he doesn't have time to teach; and I don't want to waste my time listening to him. If you're going to do it for God, give it your best effort.

Mary is sitting at the feet of Jesus listening and learning. Martha is in the kitchen. She's fixing food. She wants to be in there with Jesus and sitting beside her sister listening to the Lord teach. But you do what needs to be done. She's got at least 13 guests in her house. She's got to prepare food. You say, "Well, I would just like to sit and listen to Jesus, too." But you see, you sanctify your time. Oh, it's wonderful Mary sat and listened to Jesus, listened and learned. But what Martha is doing is potentially every bit as spiritual as what Mary was doing.

"I'm just a house wife." No, you aren't. You're far more than a house wife. My wife and I have been married 59 years. There's no way I can tell you how many meals that woman has cooked for me. And she's a wonderful cook. She can make nine different kinds of gravy out of plain water. She's a wonderful cook. But you know, I'll be hard pressed to tell you more than Easter and Christmas and Thanksgiving meals. We have basically the same thing every Easter, Christmas, and Thanksgiving, just a big spread. You always have to have deviled eggs. That's just obligatory. You always have to have biscuits. You always have to have gravy. There are certain things that are essential, but I can't tell you what she fixed for supper on Friday. All the thousands and thousands of meals that she has fixed without complaint, because she does it unto the Lord. She does it out of love. And though I can't tell you what the menu has been all these years, I can tell you it's kept me healthy. Give your talent. Use it for God, and give it your best effort.

Your Time

"Mary's not doing anything, and Martha's working," you may say. No, Mary's doing something; she's giving her time. In fact, Jesus said she's chosen for herself that good part, literally the best part, which will not be taken away from her. In English, we have the active voice, and we have the passive voice. In the New Testament language, you not only have active, as in, "I do the action," and passive, "I'm the recipient of the action," but between those two you have what is called the middle voice. It means it's of your own volition. It's up to you. The responsibility is yours. So you could really translate it as, "she has chosen for herself that good part." It's a choice you make.

We're going to forget what you serve, Martha, and you're going to forget what the menu was. But Mary's going to remember spending time with the Lord. Both are important. Both are spiritual. The Lord wants your talent, but He also wants your time.

We sang it when I was a kid: "Take time to be holy. Speak oft with thy Lord. Abide in Him always and feed on His word. By looking to Jesus, like Him thou shall be. Thy friends in thy conduct His likeness shall see."

Your Trust

I want to show you two more things that the Lord desires of us, this time in John 11. Having waited four days after receiving news about Lazarus' illness, Jesus comes from the east side of the Jordan River just before it empties into the Dead Sea, in what is now Jordan. He crosses the river; travels nineteen miles up, from twelve hundred feet below sea level to twenty-five hundred feet above sea level; crosses the Mount of Olives; and enters into their village. Finally Jesus has come to Bethany, after Lazarus has been dead for four days.

And many of the Jews came to Martha and Mary, to comfort them concerning their brother. Then Martha, as soon as she heard that Jesus was coming, went and met him: but Mary sat still in the house. Then said Martha unto Jesus, Lord, if thou hadst been here, my brother had not died. But I know, that even now, whatsoever thou wilt ask of God, God will give it thee. Jesus saith unto her, Thy brother shall rise again. Martha saith unto him, I know that he shall rise again in the resurrection at the last day. Jesus said unto her, I am the resurrection, and the life: he that believeth in me, though he were dead, yet shall he live: And whosoever liveth and believeth in me shall never die. Believest thou this? She saith unto him, Yea, Lord: I believe that thou art the Christ, the Son of God, which should come into the world. And when she had so said, she went her way, and called Mary her sister secretly, saying, The Master is come, and calleth for thee. As soon as she heard that, she arose quickly, and came unto him. Now Jesus was not yet come into the town, but was in that place where Martha met him. Now Jesus was not yet come into the town, but was in that place where Martha met him. The Jews then which were with her in the house, and comforted her, when they saw Mary, that she rose up hastily and went out, followed her, saying, She goeth unto the grave to weep there. Then when Mary was come where Jesus was, and saw him, she fell down at his feet, saying unto him, Lord, if thou hadst been here, my brother had not died.

When Jesus therefore saw her weeping, and the Jews also weeping which came with her, he groaned in the spirit, and was troubled, And said, Where have ye laid him? They said unto him, Lord, come and see. Jesus wept. — John 11:19-35

In this passage, Martha hears that Jesus is approaching the town of Bethany. Instead of waiting for Him to come, she goes to meet Him. It's not a matter of being hospitable now, but it's a matter of grief. All kinds of emotions she's had while Lazarus was sick and getting worse each day. "Jesus will come. Jesus will come." Then Jesus didn't come. Her hopes were dashed, and her grief is deep. Her brother is dead. He's been dead four days.

"Why didn't Jesus come? He's been dead now four days, my brother." In fact, it's written so strongly: "If you had been here he would not have died. My brother!" That's the way it's written, almost accusing Jesus. When Martha made this statement, the head of Jesus was touched. When Mary came later and said the exact same words, the heart of Jesus was touched. When Martha said it, "If You had been here, he would not have died, my brother," it led Him into a discussion with her on truth, and she trusted Him.

There was a myth in Judaism in those days, not Scripture but tradition, where they taught that the spirit of a person remained around that body, hovered over that body for three days waiting to see if there were any sign of life. By the fourth day, when corruption had set in and there was no sign of life, then the spirit would depart. By this time, he's corrupting. He's stinking.

But notice this conversation here. "If you had been here he would not have died, my brother," Martha says. Jesus replies, "Your brother will live again." Martha answers, "I know, he'll live again at the resurrection at the last day." You don't let what you do not know upset what you do know. "I don't know why he got sick. I don't know why You just didn't say a word from miles away and heal him. I don't know why You waited four days, but I do know he'll rise again." She's thinking of judgment. She's thinking far into the future, but Jesus is talking right

now. He led her in this conversation that calls her to have su
trust in Him. She gave this great confession. "I believe."

Jesus said, "Anybody that believes in Me shall never die. Do you believe that?" She said, "I believe You are the Christ, the Son of God that should come into the world." She's grieving, but she's trusting. Only believers can do that. Only Christians can stand at the coffin of a loved one and weep and rejoice at the same time. You don't let what you don't know upset what you do know. The Lord wants your trust even when it is the deepest of grief, and you've lost your loved one, and you can't see, you can't understand—but you can trust Him. He wants your trust, even in the times when it makes no sense.

Mary and Martha know about the healing of others. Jesus healed a girl, raised her from the dead. She was a 12-year-old girl who had only been dead a few minutes. She was still lying on the pallet where she had died, and Jesus raised her to life. He raised from the dead a young man who had been dead a few hours; by Jewish law he had to be buried before sundown, and he was being carried to the cemetery. The path of Jesus intersected with those people, and Jesus spoke to him and raised him from the dead.

A girl, 12 years old, a few minutes dead; a young man, I don't know how old, who had been dead a few hours; and now He's going to raise an adult man from the dead who had been dead for four days. Time is no problem to the One who created it. He wants you to trust.

Your Tears

Here comes Mary. She says the same thing as Martha. "If you would have been here he would not have died. My brother!" And this time it didn't touch His head. It touched His heart, and He wept.

Is Jesus not sure what He's doing to do? Oh no, He knows exactly what He's going to do. It's the compassion of Jesus. Our High Priest is not like a high priest that can't be touched with the feelings of our infirmities (Hebrews 4:15). Our High Priest can be, and He was tempted as we are, yet without sin.

There are times that I have come to the Lord with all kinds of questions, and I've just got to trust Him. There are times that I've come to the Lord when I don't even know how to say what I want to say; and though I don't cry much in public, I can do it quite well when I'm by myself with the Lord. There are times I don't even know what to say, and I weep, and He comforts me. He wants your talent, He wants your time, He wants your trust, and He wants your tears. "All your anxiety, all your care, bring to the mercy seat, leave it there. Never a burden, never a care, never a friend like Jesus."

Your Treasure

Then Jesus six days before the passover came to Bethany, where Lazarus was which had been dead, whom he raised from the dead. There they made him a supper; and Martha served: but Lazarus was one of them that sat at the table with him. Then took Mary a pound of ointment of spikenard, very costly, and anointed the feet of Jesus, and wiped his feet with her hair: and the house was filled with the odour of the ointment. Then saith one of his disciples, Judas Iscariot, Simon's son, which should betray him, Why was not this ointment sold for three hundred pence, and given to the poor? This he said, not that he cared for the poor; but because he was a thief, and had the bag, and bare what was put therein. Then said Jesus, Let her alone: against the day of my burying hath she kept this. For the poor always ye have with you; but me ye have not always. Much people of the Jews therefore knew that he was there: and they came not for Jesus' sake only, but that they might see Lazarus also, whom he had raised from the dead. But the chief priests consulted that they might put Lazarus also to death; Because that by reason of him many of the Jews went away, and believed on Jesus. — John 12:1-11

Now we come to the 12th chapter. In this chapter, six days before the Passover, Lazarus—the one who had been dead and was raised from the dead—they made him a supper that Martha served. What? Martha is doing that same thing that He had chided her for earlier. She's still cooking. She's still being the hostess with the mostest. She's still being a hospitable person. What's different? Her attitude is different.

There are two rooms: one is the kitchen, and one is in the room that you eat in, sit in, and sleep in. Outside of that, there's a little courtyard with a small wall. In those days, when you had a guest, other people would come and just watch. Even though they're not invited to the feast, they'd come and watch. Whatever's left over, they can get in on it. So there were a lot of people Martha is serving.

I have a preacher friend that I have called and said, "I want to recommend you to such and such a church." Three different times churches wanted to talk to him, and he said, "No, I'm right where God wants me, and He hasn't told me to move. Don't call anybody anymore. If ever I feel God's finished with me here, I'll call you." He's one of my heroes. You wouldn't even know his name. His church is not too large, but he's been there in the mountains for about 35 years. He's faithful. He's serving. He's doing what he did 35 years ago with the same people. The thought of preaching to the same people every week for 30 years either scares me to death or bores me to tears. I just could not do it, but that's not the call of God for me. And I don't think he could do what I do, because that's not the call of God on his life. It's about attitude. It's not just what you're doing and how long you're doing it. It's about the attitude with which you're doing it.

In chapter 12, we see Lazarus, one who is at the table with them, and then Mary, emotional Mary. Maybe this time she's helping. In my mind I see it this way. When we saw Mary in Luke 10, she was sitting at Jesus' feet. We saw her in John 11, and she came and fell down at Jesus' feet. Here she is again, in the 12th chapter of John, and she's falling down at His feet. That's a pretty good position to be in, sitting at the feet of Jesus. "Oh what words I hear Him say!" This time, in my mind, Martha is in there, too. Maybe she got some hired help. She's supervising, and she's fixing the food. Maybe Mary is helping her. They start to bring in the food to those little low tables. They're eating now, they're reclining, they're fellowshipping.

Mary is sitting there, and she looks over at her only brother. Did you notice that the 12-year-old daughter that was raised from the dead was the only daughter? And that the son of the widow was the only son? And that Lazarus is the only brother? God so loved the world that He gave His only Son, yes, but He loves everybody as though they were an only. Amen! Mary looks at her brother, not just alive but healthy, well. Whatever sickness it was is gone. He probably never looked better in all his life. She looks at him. She loves her brother. Gratitude swells up. "That's my brother. He's alive. He's well." Then she looks, and there's Jesus. She says, "That's the reason my brother is alive. Wow, what a Savior! I've got to do something."

Out of the closet under the stone she pulls out—these people had money—she pulls out a pound of nard, an ointment almost like the thickness of sap out of a tree, worth a year's salary. She could have gotten just a little bit, and it would have perfumed the whole place. But she pours it out on His feet extravagantly. Can you imagine what Jesus is thinking when He looks down at this before Him? She is giving Him her treasure. The Lord wants that. Don't be stingy with Him. I learned a long time ago you can't out give Him. "I can't afford to tithe." You can't afford not to. Give Him the treasure. When you get saved, your billfold ought to get saved too. An extravagant gift, when just a thimble full would have been sufficient.

In a marriage, in a home, you often do certain things out of logic. You do some things because they're reasonable. But if you're doing it for the Lord, you want to do it out of love. Do you love Him? She gave her treasure, an extravagant gift.

Your Testimony

Then Judas, the one who was going to betray Him, was very critical of her. "This is worth a year's salary." The whole place was perfumed. Outside everybody could smell the aroma, and Judas said, "You should have given it to the poor." It was Passover time, and you were supposed to give to the poor. But he didn't want that; he wanted the money that he could get when he sold it. And Jesus very sharply said, "Let her alone, right now! Stop that!" And then this is the testimony: "Against the day of My burying has she done this."

She didn't know she was making a picture of His death and anointing Him as you would anoint a body in death, embalming, preparing a body for burial. She just knew that her heart was overflowing with love. The Lord not only wants your treasure, but He wants your testimony.

In the passage in Luke, Lazarus is not mentioned at all. He's the central figure in John 11, and he and Mary are certainly central figures in John 12. But do you know each of them gave a testimony? In Luke 10, Mary's chosen that best part. Martha in John 11, "I believe that Thou art the Christ, the Messiah, the Son of God"—that's a testimony. In John 12, "Against the day of My burial has she done this." But Lazarus also gives a testimony, and because of him many of the Jews went away believing on Jesus.

The Lord wants your time and your talent. He wants your tears, your trust, your treasure, and your testimony. In the 12th chapter of this Gospel of John, we get a wonderful picture of what it will be like when we are with the Lord. When we're with the Lord, when we're taken out of this world, even as Lazarus was taken out of the grave and loosed—and death has a way of loosing you—when you're loosed from the pressures of problems and you're free and home with the Lord, when we are with the Lord in glorified bodies, we will do what Martha did. We will be serving the Lord.

Revelation 22, speaking of the glorified saints, says that His saints shall serve Him. I don't know what all that entails, but whatever it entails, we're going to serve the Lord. And I assure you, we'll do a better job of it there than we do here. Martha pictures that. Lazarus is sitting at the table with Him. He's fellowshipping. He's eating with the Lord. It's the marriage supper, and when we are with the Lord, we will have unbroken fellowship with Him. We shall see Him. We shall be with Him. We shall be like Him. Lazarus shows us that. And Mary, God bless her heart— here she is at the feet of Jesus again, and she is worshipping Him.

That's what we'll do in heaven. We'll worship, we'll serve, we'll fellowship with Him. I'm kind of eager for that to get started. I've served the Lord here, but I don't do as good a job here as I'll do there. I fellowship with the Lord here, but not like it will be when I see Him face-to- face. I worship Him here, but not like I shall be able to do there. Even come, Lord Jesus Christ.

Do you know what the Lord wants? Yes, He wants all six of these things—talent, time, trust, tears, treasure, and testimony. But do you know what the Lord desires? The Lord desires you. He desires me. He desires us. Submit to Him. If you're not saved, for goodness sake, for God's sake, for Christ's sake, for the sake of your family, for your own sake, get saved. Get saved now. "Oh, I'm already saved." Then the Lord wants all of those six things from you. He wants you, lock, stock, and barrel. He wants you. Yield, surrender, submit to Him. AMEN!

Chapter Nine

Satan, Christ and You
Luke 22

Satan, Christ and You
Luke 22

And the Lord said, Simon, Simon, behold, Satan hath desired to have you, that he may sift you as wheat: But I have prayed for thee, that thy faith fail not: and when thou art converted, strengthen thy brethren. — Luke 22:31-32

Both Satan and Christ desire you, the verse says. It's like football: Satan against Christ, and you're the football. Both want the football, both desire you, both bid for you, but you have to make the choice as to whose you are. Romans 6:16, tells us that we are servant to whom we yield ourselves to obey, whether of sin unto disobedience, or of obedience unto righteousness, of sin unto death, or of obedience unto righteousness. "His servants you are to whom ye yield yourselves to obey." Do you not see the conflicting powers? Both wanting you, both bidding for you, and you in the middle positioned to have the choice of which one you serve.

When you stop to think about it—coldly, not emotionally, just logically thinking about it—it is really not much of a choice. In the name of logic, why would you want to serve Satan who doesn't love you when you could serve Christ who does love you? Why would you serve one who desires to send you to hell, when you could serve the God who desires to take you to Heaven? You see, it's really not very smart not to be saved.

In this passage, there are three primary things I want to show you: the desire of Satan, the devotion of the Savior, and the duty of the Servant.

The Desire of Satan

These are strong words: "Simon, Simon, behold. Listen to

Me, Simon. Anything I'm saying is important. Look at Me, listen to Me, Simon! Satan has desired you, that he may sift you as wheat. Satan has desired to have you, a possession." From Genesis 3 through all of the Bible, we have account after account after account of the acts of Satan, of the works of Satan, of the influence of Satan, of the power of Satan, of the will of Satan, **but only three times in the Bible do we have a record of the voice of Satan.** The first is in Genesis 3 when Satan said to the woman, "Hath God said?" "God hath not said. You shall not surely die. God knows in the day you eat of this forbidden fruit you will become like gods, you will become gods, knowing good and evil." That's the first time the voice of Satan occurs.

There are two trees named in the Book of Genesis, the Tree of Life and the Tree of the Knowledge of Good and Evil. But Eve had forgotten the tree of life. Genesis 3:6, "When the woman saw the tree of the knowledge of good and evil, that it was good for food." Here, Satan appeals to the flesh. 1 John 2 says, "Love not the world, neither the things that are in the world." John goes on to describe what is "in the world," and the first thing he lists is the lust of the flesh. "When she saw the tree, that it was good for food"—that's the lust of the flesh; it appeals to her physically. "And pleasant to the eyes"—that's the lust of the eyes, and the second thing that John says is in the world. The beauty of the fruit appeals to her aesthetically. "And the tree to be desired to make one wise," not just wise, but wise as God is wise—that's the pride of life, and the third thing that John says is in the world. It appeals to her intellectually. The Bible said she did eat, and gave to her husband with her, and he did eat.

The second time the voice of Satan occurs in the Bible is not directed to a creature of God, such as Eve, but is directed to God Himself. In Job 1, Satan comes before God, and God says to Satan, "Have you considered my servant, Job? There is none like him in all the earth. Perfect, upright, hates evil, is through with evil." Satan said, "It's because You built a hedge around him. If you remove that hedge he'll curse You to Your face." The desire of Satan toward Job is the same as the desire of Satan toward Eve, which is the same as his desire toward you. He varies his tactics, his methodology, but his aim, his end, his desire is to have you. So Satan deals with Job, testing him with the same kinds of tests, the same kinds of temptations, that he tempted Eve. Satan hits Job with the loss of his possessions, the loss of his family, and the loss of his position.

The third and final time that the voice of Satan is heard in the Bible is not to a creature of God, and not to God the Father, but to God the Son. In the fourth chapter of Matthew, Satan speaks to Christ three times. Wouldn't you know that he tests Christ in the same three ways he tested Job and Eve! When you look at the temptation of Christ, he is tempted to command stones that they may be made bread. Satan takes Him to the pinnacle of the temple and says, "Cast yourself down." Then he brings him to a high mountain and shows him all the kingdoms of the world and said, "All of these will I give to you if you'll bow down and worship me." Satan has desired you so that you would worship him. He does not want you to worship God, he wants you to worship him. For he knows that God has made you in such a way that you want to worship somebody or something, and he wants to be the somebody whom you worship.

Now the lust of the flesh, the lust of the eyes, and the pride of life, whether you are talking about the temptation of Eve, the trials of Job, or the testings of Christ, they are all the same. The lust of the flesh is nothing less or nothing more than the desire to do: "Boy, I wish I could so and so." The lust of the eyes is nothing less than the desire to have: "Well, I wish I could have that." The pride of life is nothing less than the desire to be: "I wish I could be that." Satan's tactics may change—he is subtle, you know, coming as an angel of light—but his desire is always the same.

Now, let me burst your bubble. You've probably heard all your life that Satan hates you. The truth of the matter is that you're not important enough for Satan to hate. I am sorry, but that is the truth. Satan is so far greater than you and me that he's not even going to bother to hate us. We aren't important enough for Satan to hate. He hates God. Satan doesn't love anybody but himself. He doesn't hate anybody but God. His ultimate hatred is against God and anything that God loves. And because God loves you, Satan's out to get you.

I'll illustrate what I mean by a story out of my own life. I had one brother that was two years older, and one sister two years younger. When my sister was four years old she got rheumatic fever and was about to die. For 13 days and nights my mother never left the hospital room. My father would work, come home at night with us boys, send us out to relatives, and many nights spend time at the hospital because my sister was expected to die. Well, she didn't die, but then they said she would never be normal. They said she'd never be able to walk fast or run, she'd have a weak heart, and she would never be able to have children. She has two, and she retired as a lieutenant from the police force in Gadsden, Alabama.

But growing up, my sister had a hard time because of me. My daddy would whip me for something I had done wrong. I mean, he'd wear me out. And I'm smart enough to know at age 7 or 8, I can't whip my daddy, but I sure could whip my sister. And I did! Every time I'd get a whipping, my sister would get one from me. I wouldn't take a switch to her, but I would smack her. Then she'd come crying to mother, and I'd get another one, and she'd get another one. That's the way we went for years.

I went to the fifth grade and the first ten days of school I got ten whippings at school and ten whippings at home, because my sister would go home and tell them that I had gotten a whipping. She was in the third grade, and I never did find out how she knew. But every time I got a whipping at school, my sister would tell my mother, and I'd get one at home. Then she'd get one because I would whip her. I'd make her cry, tease her, tell her she was ugly, tell her she didn't have a heart, tell her hair looked like mops. I was horrible.

Now psychologically, this is called "displaced hostility" or "displaced aggression." You see, I wasn't mad at my sister. My anger was toward my daddy. But I couldn't whip my daddy, so I whipped my sister. Not because I was mad at her, but just because she was there.

Satan disobeyed, and God whipped him and drove him out of heaven. Satan knows he can't whip God, so he gets at who God loves. The reason I picked on my sister was because my parents loved her. She was the only girl, she was sick, she was the baby, and I thought I could get even with them by whipping her. My dear friend, as silly as it sounds, that's your relationship to Satan.

Now, Satan's desire is to possess people, to keep people from being saved. But once you say, "I have decided to follow Jesus" and you walk down the aisle and kneel, once you've trusted Christ, Satan knows he can't possess you. So his desire is now to thwart you in any and every way that he can. Again, he doesn't like you, and he doesn't dislike you; he hates God. Since you love God and serve Him after you are saved, he will do anything and everything he can do to keep you from being effective for God. His goal, his desire, his end is to have you that he may sift you as wheat.

In New Testament times there were two ways of separating the chaff from the wheat. One is by winnowing, the other is by sifting. They are totally different methods. After you have cut, crushed, and treaded out the grain you still have all of these hulls or husks, the chaff, mingled in with all the grain. You don't want the chaff or husk, you only want the grain. At night with the wind blowing, you shovel this wheat grain and wheat chaff both onto large sheets. People then stand around the sheets and bounce them. Both the grain and chaff go way up in the air, and the wind blows away the chaff because it's light. They do that again, and again, and again, and keep loading, and loading, and loading and that's winnowing. The wind blows away the chaff, and what is left for you to see is the good wheat. The chaff is gone.

Now, our Lord did not say, "Simon, Simon, Satan hath desired to winnow you." He said, "Satan hath desired to sift you." Sifting is an entirely different process. On a mesh-like screen, you place the kernels of wheat and the chaff. There is no wind now, so you don't throw it up in the air. What you do is you actually sift it, the same way you sift gravel when you pour concrete. When you sift, the kernels of wheat are smaller than the chaff, and the kernels of wheat fall through the grid down into the container. The only thing that is left to be seen is the chaff. The wheat is out of sight.

Do you see what He is saying? "Satan hath desired, Simon, that he may sift you." He is wanting to cover up, put out of sight any and all good that you would do or have done. He is wanting your testimony to be nothing but chaff. If you do not commit God to do the winnowing, whose fan is in His hand, if you do not let Christ do the winnowing in your life daily, and blow away the chaff so that the kernels remain, Satan will sift you. And all that will be visible is just uselessness.

Dear friend, if you are a believer, you need, you need, to keep close accounts with God. Some folks have not repented of sin in so long a time that if they ever start they are going to have to go on a fast because they won't have time to eat. How long since you have confessed sin? The Bible talks about the believer's judgment of himself. It will not be as bad at the judgment seat of Christ if we take care of our own judgment daily.

Once at the beginning of a revival, D.L. Moody invited Christians to come forward and pray for forgiveness of sin, cleansing of sin. A host of people came forward. One man knelt just near where Moody was standing, and he knelt a while. Then he got up and said to Mr. Moody, "I can't think of any sins." Moody said, "Kneel down there and guess at it!" Moody later said, "He guessed right. Every time!"

Dear friend, if you do not keep close accounts with God, Satan will sift you as wheat. What an accuser he is—the Bible says that—even so much as accusing you before the very throne in Heaven. You talk about nerve! Gall! The audacity of that, to go before God and accuse. He does! You know why? Because when he sifts all he sees is chaff, he doesn't see the wheat. "How can you claim this one as your own? Look at this chaff!"

Dear friend, I don't want anything to do with Satan's desire. I don't want him to have me. I don't want him to have any part of me. I don't want him to sift me. I would rather let God do the winnowing.

The Devotion of the Savior

"Simon, Simon, behold Satan hath desired you, but I have prayed for you." The second thing in the passage that I call to your attention is the devotion of the Savior. Isn't that precious? He says, "This is my **relationship** to you, Simon. I pray for you."

In the Old Testament, there were three offices that God ordained—prophet, priest, and king. For each of those offices, a person was anointed to become a prophet, anointed to become a priest, or anointed to become a king. The prophet stands between God and the people, but he faces the people and represents or speaks to the people for God. The priest also stands between the people and God, but he faces God and represents or speaks to God for the people. The king rules over the people under God.

Every need, *every need*—physical, medical, financial, social, spiritual, whatever—of every Old Testament Jew was met through the person and the work of the prophet, the priest, or the king. While there are instances in the Bible of persons serving in two of those capacities, such as Samuel who was both judge and priest, there is no instance in the Old Testament of one person ever serving in all three capacities.

When you come into the New Testament in the days of His flesh, Jesus was in the role of a prophet, representing God, speaking for God, speaking to the people. But having entered once into the Holy Place, He obtained eternal redemption for us. By His own blood He has purchased a better covenant. (Hebrews 9:12) He has gone and sat down. He sat down! You say, "What's so unusual about that?" In the Old Testament temple and tabernacle, there were no chairs; for the work of that priest was never finished. But when He offered one offering for sins, He sat down at the right hand of the Majesty on High, and He ever liveth to make intercession for us as our Heavenly Priest. He represents us before God. "Simon, I have prayed for you." There is one mediator between God and man, and a mediator brings peace. That's the prophet's work, but the work of intercession is His present, heavenly, priestly ministry.

"I have prayed for you, not that you'll not have tests, but that your faith fail not!" Do you think it is coincidence that Peter, in the first book that he wrote said:

That the trial of your faith, being much more precious than of gold that perisheth, though it be tried with fire, might be found unto praise and honour and glory at the appearing of Jesus Christ. — 1 Peter 1:7

"Your faith fail not," that is His **request** for us. Not that we would avoid the test, but that we would be proven in the test. Then we see his **regard** for us in the the third thing that he says.. He does not say, "And Peter *if* you ever get straightened out." He says *when*: "When thou art converted."

Now dear friend, "converted" is a word that we misuse more often than we use correctly. We say a persn got converted meaning that person got saved. That's not true. A person doesn't get converted when they get saved. The word "converted" literally means "to turn again, to turn another way." What our Lord is praying for Simon is, "Simon, when you are turned again." "Simon, before the cock crows you are going to deny me three times."

That's exactly what they talked about in the very next verses. The Lord knew what Simon was going to do even though Simon said, "Though all men leave Thee, I'll never leave Thee. I'm not going to be ashamed of you. If everybody denies You, I'll never deny You." Our Lord said, "Before the cock crows you are going to deny Me three times. You are going down, down, deep down, deep into a valley. But Simon, you are not going to stay there. When you are turned again…" What regard He has for us!

"Pray for me, Brother Mathews, I don't know if I'm going make it or not." Oh friend, you are going to make it. "I just don't know if I can stand much more." Well, if God knows you can't stand much more He is not going to give you much more. "I just don't see how I'll make it." I'll tell you how you make it; you make it the same way you've made it this far—by faith.

The Duty of the Servant

The third thing we see in this passage is the duty of the servant. "Strengthen thy brethren." You may think that is kind of anti-climactic. "When you are turned again, Peter, preach the sermon at Pentecost in Acts 2." That's not what He said. "When you are converted, heal the man that sets at the beautiful gate in Acts 3." That's not what He said. "When you are converted, Peter, become the leader of the New Testament Church." That's not what He said, "When you are converted, Peter, let signs and miracles be done by you so that people will desire your shadow to pass over them." No, that's not what He said. But "strengthen thy brethren" seems almost anti-climactic, doesn't it?

Dear friend, if you think that way, it shows you how little regard you have for the brethren. I am amazed, I am appalled at how little regard most believers have for the Body of Christ, that we would dissect it and divide it and split it. God, have mercy on us. "When thou art converted, strengthen thy brethren." That is not anti-climactic. No, that is the zenith of it!

"Peter, Peter, Simon, Simon, when you are turned again, strengthen your brethren." I wonder why? Why would He say such a thing? **First because of the example that Christ gave for us.** Do you love your church like Christ loved the Church? How is that for an example? Do you love the church like Christ loved His Church and gave Himself for it? What are you willing to give for your church? He left us an example that we should follow in His steps (1 Peter 2:21). Let this mind be in you which was also in Christ Jesus, who being in the form of God thought it not robbery to be equal with God, but made Himself of no reputation. (Phil. 2:6) Isn't it odd that we worry about our reputation and He made Himself of none? He eventually, being found and fashioned as a man, humbled Himself and became obedient unto death, even the death on the cross. (Phil. 2:8)

Brethren, if God so loved us, we ought also to love one another. Strengthen thy brethren. Why? "Because of the example that I'm setting for you," that's what He's saying. Strengthen thy brethren.

Second, we are to strengthen the brethren because we are brethren. A brother or sister in the Lord is not our enemy. We are part of the same family. Our enemy is the Devil, not another believer. It is sad, but often the unsaved people show more love than those who are saved. In the USA, especially, we do not put enough emphasis on the fellowship within the family. One of the "benefits" of being saved is that we have access into the family. When Peter admonishes us "above all, have fervent love among yourselves," he is highlighting fellowship. In truth, Jesus did not die just to allow us entrance into heaven, but to enjoy fellowship on the way there.

Third, we are strengthen the brethren because we all need it. Without the fellowship, we would live isolated, lonely lives. When we attend services, we should have already prayed, "Lord, bless me today by making me a blessing." Such a prayer would have a great affect upon our church services and upon our lives.

Fourth, strengthen the brethren because what we do to one another, we do to the Lord. In essence, when you bad-mouth a believer, you are doing it "as unto the Lord." When you criticize a believer, it affects Him. We are members of His Body, flesh of His flesh, bone of His bone; we are members in particular. He is the Head over the Body, and you think if you hurt this finger it doesn't hurt the Head? The pain is felt in the head and sends the message back so the finger can hurt. "What you've done unto the least of these, my brethren, you've done it unto Me."

Fifth, strengthen the brethren because what we do to others, we do to ourselves. If I strive to fulfill the "one anothers" of the Scripture, I am strengthening myself as well as strengthening others. If I show such things as love, graciousness, and forgiveness to another, I have not reduced my supply of those characteristics. Rather, I have increased them. Similarly, if I harbor harsh feelings toward someone and express those feelings, I have not reduced, but rather increased those feelings.

We may all be strengtheners! Age, health, wealth, education, how long we have been believers--none of those are variables in our strengthening potential. We may not be pastors or teachers, but we may all be strengtheners! AMEN!

Chapter Ten

The Wonder of the World to Come
Isaiah 35

The Wonder of the World to Come
Isaiah 35

I am going to tell you about a wonderful world that is to come, but everything that I tell you applies specifically, exclusively, to people who know Christ as their Savior. This message does not speak comfort to people who are unsaved. If you want to participate, if you want to be a citizen of the wonderful world which is to come, then you must be born again.

The wonderful world which is to come will be created new, fresh, just for Christian people. So everything I tell you in the next few pages is for the edification and the encouragement of the believer.

If you are unsaved, you are like a little boy standing outside on a sidewalk looking through the window, with his nose pressed against the glass, looking in at a candy store and not having a penny to buy a piece of candy. What he doesn't know is that all of the candy is free. And I hope to God that I can describe it in such a way that you will want to become a citizen of this country; that you will want to repent of your sins and trust Christ as your own personal Savior.

The wilderness and the solitary place shall be glad for them; and the desert shall rejoice, and blossom as the rose. It shall blossom abundantly, and rejoice even with joy and singing: the glory of Lebanon shall be given unto it, the excellency of Carmel and Sharon, they shall see the glory of the LORD, and the excellency of our God. Strengthen ye the weak hands, and confirm the feeble knees. Say to them that are of a fearful heart, Be strong, fear not: behold, your God will come with vengeance, even God with a recompence; he will come and save you. Then the eyes of the blind shall be opened, and the ears of the deaf shall be unstopped. Then shall the lame man leap as an hart, and the tongue of the dumb sing: for in the wilderness shall waters break out, and streams in the desert. And the parched ground shall become a pool, and the thirsty land springs of water: in the habitation of dragons, where each lay, shall be grass with reeds and rushes. And an highway shall be there, and a way, and it shall be called The way of holiness; the unclean shall not pass over it; but it shall be for those: the wayfaring men, though fools, shall not err therein. No lion shall be there, nor any ravenous beast shall go up thereon, it shall not be found there; but the redeemed shall walk there: And the ransomed of the LORD shall return, and come to Zion with songs and everlasting joy upon their heads: they shall obtain joy and gladness, and sorrow and sighing shall flee away. — Isaiah 35:1-10

You'll never read anything more beautiful than that. But **this wonderful world of Isaiah 35 will not come based upon the word and the work of man.** Rather, it will be ushered in by the word and the work of almighty God. In other words, the world of Isaiah 35 will not come based upon what man or society does, but it will be based upon what God has said and what God will do. All of the efforts of man to establish a utopia have ended in utter futility. From the Greek philosophers of Socrates, Plato, and Aristotle, and particularly in the Republic, there have always been formalized treatises written describing what a perfect world would be like.

We're hearing now in our world things like, "What we need is a one-world government. What we need is a one-world monetary system. What we need is a one-world language. And if ever we can get a one-world government, a one world monetary system, and a one-world language, we will be able to talk. We will be able to have economic stabilization and a fair distribution of wealth. Everybody will understand everybody else, and everybody will have the same rules governing them. We will bring in a world of peace."

I want you to know that's not true, and it never has been true, and it never will be true. In fact, what I have described to you is Genesis 11. In Genesis 11, before the Tower of Babel was built, the world was of one government, one language, and one monetary system. They had then what many would like to have now, and God destroyed their efforts to build a temple. He scattered the people and confused their tongues.

The world of Isaiah 35 will not come based upon the work of man. Regardless of whether the efforts of man are in the area of religion, philosophy, education, science, human government, military affairs, or whatever other discipline or area of human knowledge you would pursue. All of the collective wisdom of man, all of the collective efforts of man, and all of the collective desires of man will never be able to bring in a world of Isaiah 35. So long as men are born with sinful natures, they will never be able to bring in a perfect world. Like begets like, and sinners beget sinners. And if your daddy was a sinner, you're a sinner. And if you're a sinner, your child is going to be born with the same sinful nature and the same tendency to sin. As long as people are born with a sinful nature, they will never be able to bring in a world like Isaiah 35.

The idea of the communes sprang up in the 1960s in this country, and everybody was amazed at the communes. There are still a few around. The idea was that everybody would live on the commune, bring their share, and share alike. And you see this way of living all over Israel. From the Zionists to the Socialists there have these communes, though they don't call them communes.

It's not a new idea. Following the Revolutionary War, you may be interested to know, there were communes that sprang up all along the eastern coast. Nathanial Hawthorne lived in one, and some of the most brilliant minds of that early era of our country lived in the commune with Nathanial Hawthorne. In writing about it, Hawthorne said, "We had the most intelligent potatoes in all New England, except nobody knew how to grow them." Their plans for the commune and utopia disappeared within three years.

All of the efforts of man will never bring in a world of Isaiah 35. I have lived long enough to know of the New Deal and the Great Society, and this deal, and that deal, and all of the others. While I appreciate all the efforts that people put forth from a sincere heart to improve the welfare of humanity, they will never be able to wipe out poverty. We will never be able to wipe out ignorance. We will never be able to wipe out selfishness, sin, and crime. With all of our learning, we have never solved the two basic problems of sin and death—and that's the problem. The problem is not poverty. The problem is not ignorance and illiteracy. The problem is sin and death, and we've never solved them. We shall never solve those problems.

So Isaiah 35 will not be brought in by the efforts of man. Instead, it shall be brought in by this word of God, by God keeping His promises made in His word.

The second statement that must be said before we come to Isaiah 35 is that **things are going to get worse before they get better.** That's putting it succinctly and briefly. But before Isaiah 35 can come—a world of utopia—before it happens, the time of Isaiah 35 will be preceded by a time of woe and trouble and affliction and tribulation, such as there has not been since the beginning of the world. The Bible says so. Before the Millennium of Isaiah 35, before a one thousand year reign of Christ literally upon this earth, before King Jesus reigns, that period of thousand years will be preceded by days that the Bible calls tribulation; seven years of tribulation like the world hasn't seen since it began, the Bible says. It will be a day unlike anything that the world has ever known.

You can take your Bible and read Revelation chapter 6 to chapter 19. All of those chapters of the Book of the Revelation are devoted to a 7-year period of human history that mankind will undergo when the Holy Spirit, will be taken out of this world. Then, the spirit of anti-Christ and the devil himself will be turned loose on this earth as he has never been before. Men will be unrestrained and will give full vent to all of their sinful nature.

Thank God, I'm not going to be here when it happens. For

Rapture

before the Millennium, there comes the Tribulation, and before the Tribulation there comes an event that is called the Blessed Hope. It is the glorious appearing of our great God and Savior. It's called the Rapture. "For the Lord Himself shall descend from heaven with a shout, with the voice of the archangel, and with the trump of God: and the dead in Christ shall rise first: then we which are alive and remain shall be caught up together with them in the clouds to meet the Lord in the air: and so shall we ever be with the Lord. Wherefore, comfort one another with these words." (1 Thessalonians 4:16-18)

I am glad that I will not be here during those grave days of tribulation. This is the calendar of events. Some golden daybreak Jesus will come. I don't know when. It could be today. It could be tomorrow. Do you know how I know He's coming? It's because He hasn't come yet. That's exactly how I know. When He went away He said, "I will come again." He hasn't come, has He? So that's how I know He's coming. I have known Him since 1947. He has never lied to me, not one time. I believe everything He's ever told me, and when we read the Book, He said, "I will come again and receive you unto Myself, that where I am, there you may be also." (John 14:3) Because He hasn't come, I'm still here. Because He hasn't come, I know He's coming. When He comes, I'm going with Him. This mortal will put on immortality. I will be changed in an instant. In the twinkling of an eye I will be with a new body like unto our Lord's glorious body. (1 Corinthians 15:52) That could happen at any moment. That's the imminent return of Jesus Christ.

You say, "If you really believe that, you ought to go off and sit down on a rock somewhere and wait for the Lord to come." No, that's dumb. I am not told just to wait. I am told to work. I am told to occupy until He comes. It is my obligation unto God to keep what He has entrusted unto me, and to do my best with whatever abilities He has given me, to do what I can. I am to do two things: **to evangelize the unsaved and to edify the saints.** That's all. I live a very simple life. I have dedicated myself to three things: **(1) to evangelize the unsaved, (2) to edify Christians, and (3) to encourage pastors.** That's all I do.

That's my whole life. Because I believe the Lord is coming, I am not to sit down and wait for Him to come. I am to be working, I am to be busy, I am to be busy at His business, I am to live like a Christian, I am to encourage other Christians, I am to try to enlist other people in the call of Christ.

If I had ten thousand lives to give, I would give every one of them to Christ. I don't want to trade places with anybody. I really don't. I feel sorry for every physician I know because every patient he treats dies. Think about it. Eventually, everybody he treats will die. But anybody who will take the medicine that I prescribe will never die. I wouldn't trade places with anybody.

The Lord is coming. When the saints leave, then come those days of the Tribulation upon the earth. After those seven years, the Lord comes back visibly, and His feet shall stand that day on the Mount of Olives. His feet will stand that day on the Mount of Olives. He shall walk down the sides of the Mount of Olives. He will walk across the Kidron Valley. He will walk up the sides of that eastern slope, through those eastern gates. He will walk into the rebuilt temple, and He will sit down upon the throne of David. For 1,000 years, He will reign in peace and righteousness upon this earth.

When He comes back to this earth, I shall come back with Him. It's not because I'm special but because I'm His. When He comes back, every believing child of God comes with Him, and we will enter into that Millennial reign, into that 1,000 year reign of Christ. Now, what will that world be like? There are **five things** I want to tell you about the wonderful world which is to come.

A Politically Perfect World

The world which is to come will be perfect. Politically, it will be perfect. Who shall be reigning over this earth? King Jesus will reign.

Jesus shall reign where'er the sun
Does his successive journeys run,
His kingdom stretch from shore to shore
Till moons shall wax and wane no more.

He will reign as supreme ruler. Under Him are people who are in positions of authority, ruling based upon faithful service to the Lord. The Bible says:

His lord said unto him, Well done, thou good and faithful servant: thou hast been faithful over a few things, I will make thee ruler over many things: enter thou into the joy of thy lord. — Matthew 25:21

When our Lord reigns from Jerusalem, those who have been faithful to Him will have positions of authority and leadership throughout all of this earth. Now, imagine living in a world where everybody who is in any position of authority, every governmental leader, every person from the dog catcher to the President, from the magistrate right on up, every person who is in any position of authority is as perfect as Jesus Himself. Can you imagine that? There is not that situation today. That's why we have repeated elections. That's why some are voted out and some are voted in, because they are not perfect. Try as they may to do their best, they're not perfect. And some of them are not honest. Many of them are. I suspect most of them are basically honest, but they're not perfect.

However, the day is going to come when King Jesus reigns in rigteousness and in justtice, and every person who is in any position of authority under Him will be just as perfect as He is. That's going to be marvelous. We question the decisions of our government, and sometimes we should. But in King Jesus' government, you'll not need to question any decision. It will all be perfect politically.

A Geographically Perfect World

Secondly, the wonderful world which is to come will be perfect from the standpoint of its geography. It will be geographically perfect. A word that has come into vogue in the last few years is that word ecology. It is the word of the relation of living things with other living things. Its meaning is now to the relation of one thing to another thing, whether living or not. It involves

120

air, water, soil, space, matter, and time. It involves human kind, animal life, and plant life. It seemingly involves anything and everybody. If you don't know what it is and it's so big you don't know what to call it, call it ecology. You'd probably be right.

But our world is not perfect geographically. We have tornados, earthquakes, hurricanes, and cyclones. We have droughts, famines, and volcanic eruptions. We have all kinds of upheavals of nature. Do you not know that this world is under the same curse that man is? The Bible says that the world was placed under a curse, that the whole creation groans and travails together in pain until now, waiting for the manifestation of the sons of God.

So when you hear of the earthquakes, tornados, floods, and all of the upheavals of weather, all of the upheavals of nature, you're hearing a creation that's groaning and travailing in pain, waiting for the day when King Jesus makes every wrong right, every crooked straight. All creation waits for that day. One day, the world will be perfect geophysically. The geophysical world will be perfect. He says in chapter 35:

The wilderness and the solitary place shall be glad for them; and the desert shall rejoice, and blossom as the rose. It shall blossom abundantly, and rejoice even with joy and singing: the glory of Lebanon shall be given unto it, the excellency of Carmel and Sharon, they shall see the glory of the LORD, and the excellency of our God. — Isaiah 35:1-2

I want to show you the extent to which God the Father will go to make this new world to our liking. He does not name cities but regions. When you say Lebanon, you're talking northern Palestine. You are talking cedars. You're talking mountains. You're talking cool breezes, deep valleys, tall mountains. Poor Lebanon, what used to be called the Pearl of the Middle East is now devastated. It has been battered back and forth by everything around it. But when our Lord talks about Lebanon, He's talking about a mountainous area, green hills, clear crystal streams. The glory of Lebanon shall be given unto it. I'm a mountaineer. I was born a mountaineer. I like the mountains. I'd like to live in that part of the country during the millennium.

And then He says, "The excellency of Carmel." That's the seacoast. He's talking beaches. He's talking fish. He's talking sand. He's talking sea breeze. There are some folks who think that they haven't lived a year unless they've gone to the beach and burned up in the sun. I think that's silly, but that's all right. Not everybody has the good sense to choose the mountains.

So there are folks who like the mountains, and there are folks who like the seashore, and then there are folks who like flatland. There are actually people in Kansas who like it. I don't care what you say, Kansas is 10,000 miles long. I have driven across it. It is pathetic, just straight. Whereas in the mountains you have the wood and the timber, in the flatlands you have the vegetables and the fruits. When the Bible speaks of Sharon, it's talking about one valley that is 15 miles wide and 40 miles long. Right now, they grow and harvest three crops a year.

So you have mountains, and you have seashore, and you have flatland. You say, "Well, that's nothing." I think it shows the extent to which the Lord is going to go to make the world to the liking for His own children. Imagine, if you will, living in a world where there is absolutely no fear of any danger of a forest fire, of a sand storm, of a flood, or of a tornado. None. Where there is absolutely nothing to fear weather-wise. The geophysical world will be at peace with itself.

I remind you, if you are unsaved, this world that I am describing is not for you. It is only for those who know the Lord. They are what this Bible calls the "redeemed of the Lord," the "ransomed of the Lord." And if you want to live in a world like this, you're going to have to get saved. It's not for you in your lost condition.

A World of Perfect People

In the third place, the world itself will be perfect from the standpoint that the people who are inhabiting that world will themselves be physically perfect. There are folks who, before reading this, had to take a pill for their high blood pressure, some had to give themselves an insulin shot, some had to take a dose of Valium or Librium, some had to take medicine for kidney problems, or back problems, and on and on.

> *Then shall the eyes of the blind be opened. Then shall the ears of the deaf be unstopped. Then shall the tongue of the mute sing. The lame man, the crippled body, shall leap as a wild deer. — Isaiah 35:6*

I never have enough time. It seems like I'm always battling with time. But in that age, I won't have to go to the airport and fly to Pittsburgh and wait 2 hours, and then fly to New York and catch a 747, and go to Tel Aviv, and then catch a bus and go up to Jerusalem. I'll be going instantly. I'll be standing here and say, "I want to go to Jerusalem and see the King," and instantly I'll be there. You say, "I don't believe that." You just get in the Millennium and hang onto my coat tail and I'll show you.

Jesus in His resurrected body had the ability to appear and disappear. The first time they saw Him, He came through the doors; and the doors were shut. I'll be able to have a body like that. Blessed be God.

A Spiritually Perfect World

Also, it'll be a world of spiritual perfection. I imagine living in a world where there is no Satan. When King Jesus comes back to this earth, He will bind Satan and cast him into the sides of the bottomless pit for the duration of that Millennial kingdom. Imagine living in a world where there will be no temptation, no solicitation to think evil, to say evil, to hear evil, and to do evil.

I'll tell you who gives me the most spiritual problems. I do. I am not what I was; I am not what I am going to be, thank God, and I am so far short of what I want to be. But when I meet my Lord and I get a body like His, and I am finally free of this old nature, I will be like Him. I will not think evil. I will not speak evil. I will not hear evil. I will not do evil. I will be spiritually perfect. We'll see Him as He is. Praise the Lord! It will be a world of spiritual perfection. In verses 8, 9, and 10, He talks about it.

And an highway shall be there, and a way, and it shall be called The way of holiness; the unclean shall not pass over it; but it shall be for those: the wayfaring men, though fools, shall not err therein. No lion shall be there, nor any ravenous beast shall go up thereon, it shall not be found there; but the redeemed shall walk there: And the ransomed of the LORD shall return, and come to Zion with songs and everlasting joy upon their heads: they shall obtain joy and gladness, and sorrow and sighing shall flee away. — *Isaiah 35:8-10*

Peter says it this way:

Be sober, be vigilant; because your adversary the devil, as a roaring lion, walketh about, seeking whom he may devour: whom resist stedfast in the faith, knowing that the same afflictions are accomplished in your brethren that are in the world. But the God of all grace, who hath called us unto his eternal glory by Christ Jesus, after that ye have suffered a while, make you perfect, stablish, strengthen, settle you. — *1 Peter 5:8-10*

Imagine what it's going to be like when you don't have to resist the devil, because he's not around. We will be spiritually perfect. Think about it.

I'll never again have to get down on my face before God and confess a sin. I wonder if the Lord grows as weary hearing them as I do confessing them. "Lord, I've failed. I messed up again. I acted in the flesh. I'm sorry." How many times has He heard me say it? And I get tired of saying it, but I have to say it, because I keep messing up. But blessed be God, one of these days prayer will be a thing of the past, and praise will take the place of prayer. And faith will be a thing of the past. Man, you don't need faith when you've got sight. I'll see Him face to face.

A Psychologically Perfect World

Finally, it will be a world of psychological perfection. The passage said:

Say to them that are of a fearful heart, Be strong, fear not.
— Isaiah 35:4

That's psychological. We fear everything in this country. From heart failure to crop failure, we fear it all. There was a day when I was a kid that we never locked the doors on the house. In fact, one time we were going away on vacation, and my daddy said, "I guess we ought to lock the house." But we couldn't find the key. We left for 2 weeks with the house unlocked. You don't do that now. You're silly if you do. Imagine having a world of absolutely nothing to fear. With what can I compare it? There's nothing with which I can compare it, because you don't have any basis to start with. You don't know what it is to live in a world where there's nothing to fear. But in that world, there will be absolutely nothing to fear. It'll be a fearless world. The very thought of it is foreign to us. There will be nothing to fear.

And the ransomed of the LORD shall return, and come to Zion with songs and everlasting joy upon their heads: they shall obtain joy and gladness, and sorrow and sighing shall flee away. — Isaiah 35:10

Joy is psychological. Gladness is psychological. Sorrow is psychological. Sighing is psychological. All of those are psychological. I don't care who you are, how good a Christian you are, how moral, upright, how pure, etc. If you would let me ask the questions one on one—and you promised to answer them truthfully—within five minutes, I would ask questions and solicit answers from you that would embarrass you. There is not a man or woman who doesn't live with regrets. Those are sorrows. They may have been sins that you committed and confessed to God. You forsook them, and God forgave you of them. God forgot them. He never remembers them against you anymore, but the devil will not let you forget them.

125

Every person has regrets. I don't care how good you are, you've said things, done things, and been things that you regret. Everybody lives with that. And when you're ready to do something for the Lord, here comes the devil who says, "You don't have a right to be here. Who are you?" You'll live with that. You have to recommit it to the Lord. "Lord, I don't want the devil to defeat me in this area," and the Lord says, "I forgave you of it 15 years ago." "But I can't forget it because the devil won't let me forget it." It's like a millstone hung around your neck, and you live with it as long as you're on this earth.

Everybody has regrets, things for which he is sorry. But imagine living in a world where there is absolutely no remembrance of anything bad, where you have absolutely nothing to be sorry about, where you have nothing to regret. No sorrow. No regrets. No remorse. In all my counseling through the years, we get down to business when the statement comes out one of two ways: "if only I had" or "if only I had not." Many of the problems in counseling are attributed to those two statements. All of the emotional upheaval coming out of what has happened in the past, the person can't adjust to it, can't get over it, can't forget it. The regret is there gnawing away at their emotional vitality. It's just zapping them of their strength. There's coming a day, child of God, when every bit of that will gone. Sorrow will flee away.

Then He said "sighing." It is such a strong word in the Hebrew. The only way I can render it is "heartbreaking agony." Have you lived long enough to have heartbreaking agony? Have you lived long enough to have such an experience that has so devastated you that all you can do is just groan? It'll flee away.

Heartbreaking agony is what the preacher hears when he goes to the home to tell the family that the father has dropped dead. I have done that more than once. It's not a fun thing. It's the denial that you hear. "No! It can't be!" And then there's wailing. That's heartbreaking agony. It's the sound that you hear at the committal service at the graveside when the widow has cried for three days. There's nothing more to cry, and yet she just bawls. I have never felt so helpless in my life as when the funeral director says, "That concludes the service. You may now return to your cars." You shake hands with the widow and with the children. Your heart breaks with them. The wailing is over, and they are empty and numb.

My father died in 1964. After the funeral, my brother and sister went to their homes. I was with my mother for a few nights. I was in one bedroom, and she was in the other. About 2 o'clock in the morning I woke up and I thought, "I hear groaning." I lay there and listened. It was not sobbing; it was coming from deep within her heart. Without turning on the light I got out of bed and walked out to the hall and into her bedroom. The door was open, and there was no light on. I stood there in the darkness, and then I sat down on the bed. When I did, she stirred. I reached out said, "Mother, are you all right? You were groaning." She said, "I'm sorry I woke you." I asked, "What's wrong, Mother?" She said, "Son, I have cried until I can't cry anymore. I want to cry but the well of tears is dry, and it seems like all I can do is groan. I drop off to sleep, and, as I did for 30-some years, I roll over to put my arm around him; but he's not here. I'm just about to die, and I can't help it. It's just groaning." That's heartbreaking agony.

One of these days that will flee away. Imagine a thousand years of never hearing, "Pray for brother so-and-so who's sick. Pray for my son who has cancer. Pray for our 13-year-old boy who has a brain tumor. Pray for our 10-year-old son who's undergoing kidney surgery. Pray for so-and-so who was hurt in an accident from a fall from a horse, and has head injuries." Imagine living in a world where there won't be any of that, and there is nothing to sorrow about, and there is no heartbreak. All of that will be gone, and if you listen closely you can hear, "And the ransomed of the Lord shall return and come to Zion with songs." I think I can hear them. Can you hear them?

It's going to be a wonderful world with songs and everlasting joy upon their heads. It's a concept that is totally foreign to us, everlasting joy. You've been in places where you feel like all you have to do is take one step up and you'll have your own private rapture. But then thirty minutes later, the devil is giving you a hard time. I have preached the Gospel and seen the altar lined; and then I look back and remember others who could not make a move to trust Christ, and my joy was gone.

But the joy that comes, He's talking about everlasting joy. He's talking about joy that is uninterrupted, joy undiluted, not joy mixed with sorrow. Just joy, joy unending.

What a world that is going to be like! I'm glad I'm saved. I'll tell you again, if you are not saved, this wonderful world which I've spoken of is not for you. The only way you're going to be there is if you trust Christ as your Savior. **There's one other thing I must tell you.** What I have talked about in Isaiah 35 is the Millennial world, and as good as it is, that's not heaven. Heaven's better than that! AMEN!

Chapter Eleven

You've Said, "Amen." Now What?
Romans 16

You've Said, "Amen." Now What?
Romans 16

We say "amen" as an expression of agreement. The preacher says something, and you say "amen." Or you say it at the end of a prayer. It is one of the universal words. I have heard it on five different continents. In China, one man prayed, and when he said a phrase, everybody said, "Amin!" He said another phrase, and everybody said, "Amin!" When I stood up and turned around and looked, there were tears rolling down their cheeks. He was praying, and they were right with him. We say "amen" as a statement of agreement. Jesus loves the little children. Amen! We agree with what's said.

When a person says "amen" at the end of his prayer, he is saying, "That's it." The word means "it's settled," "let it be," or "as it has been stated." It's over. It's done. Go to the last chapter of the Bible, and John closes the book of the Revelation:

And the Spirit and the bride say, Come. And let him that heareth say, Come. And let him that is athirst come. And whosoever will, let him take the water of life freely. — Revelation 22:17

In verse 20, Jesus is speaking at the beginning, and then John responds.

He which testifieth these things saith, Surely I come quickly. Amen. Even so, come, Lord Jesus. — Revelation 22:20

Jesus said, "Surely I come quickly." John said, "Even so, come, Lord Jesus." Who said the "amen" between them? Do you think John said it? Do you think the Lord said it? If the Lord said it, He said, "Surely I come quickly. Amen. That's it. I'm finished speaking. It's over." If John said it, he spoke in agreement, "Yes, amen. Even so, come, Lord Jesus." That same word can be used in two different ways.

Now come to Romans 16. Every epistle, every letter of Paul, ends basically the same way. "And the grace of our Lord Jesus Christ be with you all, amen." Or, "grace and peace from the Lord Jesus Christ, amen." The book of Hebrews ends the same way. Every one of these epistles ends with an "amen," and so does Romans. But in Romans, Paul ends a little differently.

Salute one another with an holy kiss. The churches of Christ salute you. — Romans 16:16

You think he's finished, but then he continues.

And the God of peace shall bruise Satan under your feet shortly. The grace of our Lord Jesus Christ be with you. Amen. — Romans 16:20

You think he's finished because that's generally how he ends all of his letters. "The grace of our Lord Jesus Christ be with you. Amen." But he goes on.

Timotheus my workfellow, and Lucius, and Jason, and Sosipater, my kinsmen, salute you. I Tertius, who wrote this epistle, salute you in the Lord. Gaius mine host, and of the whole church, saluteth you. Erastus the chamberlain of the city saluteth you, and Quartus a brother. The grace of our Lord Jesus Christ be with you all. Amen. — Romans 16:21-24

Now he's finished. Right? He's said "amen," but he's not finished. So what do you do after you say "amen"?

Now to him that is of power to stablish you according to my gospel, and the preaching of Jesus Christ, according to the revelation of the mystery, which was kept secret since the world began, But now is made manifest, and by the scriptures of the prophets, according to the commandment of the everlasting God, made known to all nations for the obedience of faith: To God only wise, be glory through Jesus Christ forever. Amen. — Romans 16:25-27

Do you ever say "amen"? You ought to. Less and less Christians are saying "amen." We've about reached the point in Christian churches where you almost have to give lessons. But sometimes "amen" is not enough. The next time, after you've said "amen," say, "Praise the Lord!" Then, sometimes that's still not enough; sometimes you want to say, "Hallelujah!" Have you ever done that? Amen! Praise the Lord! Hallelujah! What's left to say after "amen"? The only thing left is, "Glory!"

I want to ask five questions about "glory." The first one I shall not be able to answer, but neither will you. The second is a harder question, but not as hard to answer. The third one is not as hard. The fourth is easy. And the last one is so easy that one word, and we'll be finished.

"The church of Christ salute you. The grace of our Lord Jesus Christ be with you. Amen." But he can't stop, and so he gives a doxology. "Doxa" is the most common New Testament word for glory. So we sing the Doxology: "Praise God from whom all blessings flow."

What is Glory?

"To God [that's who] be glory [what] through Jesus Christ [how] for ever [when]." (Romans 16:27) If we back up a couple of verses, Romans 16:25-26 tell us why glory is to be given to God: because of who He is and because of what He does. What is glory? I have probably spent the last 10 years and about 150 hours trying to define and fully comprehend the word "glory." There are certain words that are just tremendously huge. One is grace. The other is glory. How do you define glory? There are thirteen Hebrew forms of the word in the Old Testament and nine forms of the Greek word in the New Testament that are translated as "glory." It is used of people, things, and even places; it is used as a noun, as a verb, and as an adjective. It's used to refer to both external and internal glory.

Matthew 6:29 says, "And yet I say unto you, That even Solomon in all his glory was not arrayed like one of these." That's external. It's an expression of praise, like when you say, "Amen! Praise the Lord! Hallelujah! Glory!" It's an expression of joy. It's a verb. Galatians 6:14, on the other hand, shows internal glory: "God forbid that I should glory [boast] save in the cross of our Lord Jesus Christ." It's such a big word, and there are so many different meanings of the word.

Interestingly enough, the first time the word "glory" appears in the Bible, it is referring to a man, an unbeliever even. In Genesis 31:1, when the sons of Laban complained that Jacob had taken the glory of their father, it speaks of his importance, his status, and his stature. He's a shepherd, and yet this Jacob has come in and taken the glory of their father. The last time it's used in the Bible is in Revelation 21:26 when, in the kingdom, the nations of the earth shall bring their glory unto Him in Jerusalem—glory of the pagan nations brought to a holy God. The word is used to refer to both believers and unbelievers.

In chapter 4 of this book, I explained that the external reference to the word glory indicates size, like the vastness of space and the galaxies. Imagine you were standing at the edge of space. You look out, and what do you see? More space. The heavens declare the glory of God, and there's no end to it!

The word can mean weight. The word can mean light. The word can mean brilliance and splendor. There are so many shades of meaning to the word. We often use it in such limited ways. If we say, "Glory!" we're praising God. If we say, "You can't glory in that," we use it to boast or brag.

Two times in the New Testament is it used as "glorious." One of those times is in Romans 8 when it speaks "of the glorious liberty of the sons of God." The other time is even more precious. "Glorious" is used to describe the church, the only time in the New Testament where a descriptive adjective is used before the word "church." "That Christ may present unto Himself a glorious church without spot or wrinkle." (Ephesians 5:27) All of the other adjectives for the church are locative, referring to a location or place: the church at Corinth, the church at Thessalonica, the church at Rome, the church of Galatians.

I can't answer the question "what is glory?" But I can tell you that I have read and read, out of my library and out of other pastors' libraries, and each time I go look for the word "glory." I've read rabbinical writings and about everything I can get my hands on. My head swims. It's just too much! It overwhelms me, and I just have to say, "I can't do it." You can't define that word. It's like a diamond. Every way you turn it, there's a different facet. What is glory? We want to interpret it as praise to God, but it's so much more. It's a wonderful word, and I apologize for not being able to explain it more fully. If you want to spend minutes, hours, days, weeks, months, and years, just take the word "glory" and dig in.

Why Should Glory be Given to God?

Our second question is easier to answer: why is glory to be given to God?

To God only wise, be glory through Jesus Christ for ever. Amen. — Romans 16:27

Now to him that is of power to stablish you according to my gospel, and the preaching of Jesus Christ, according to the revelation of the mystery, which was kept secret since the world began. — Romans 16:25

"Kept secret since the world began"—Oh, what a phrase! Do you know that you understand and take for granted things that the angels themselves desire to look into? There's not an Old Testament prophet that saw the Church Age. They didn't see it. They wrote prophecies and asked, "What does that mean?" They didn't know. You don't see the Church Age in the Old Testament. They saw the First Coming, they saw the Second Coming, but they didn't see anything in between. It's a mystery, not something out of the twilight zone but something that's not yet revealed.

134

In Ephesians 3, Paul says, "The mystery was revealed unto me." That Jew and Gentile are placed together in Christ and made one new man—this mystery was hid throughout the ages since the world began, and angels don't know and understand this mystery. The Bible says there's rejoicing in the presence of the angels over one sinner that repents. Everybody says this means that the angels rejoice, but it doesn't mean that at all. Angels would have no reason to rejoice. They don't know what salvation is. They might look at you and say, "Good for him."

Now, when Jesus said that, where was Jesus? He was on the earth. Jesus, on this earth, said there is rejoicing in the presence of the angels over one sinner that repents. Who's in heaven? God the Father. Who is it that rejoices? It's God the Father, not the angels. Think about it. Who else is up there? The righteous of the Old Testament were still in Sheol. "Today you shall be with me in paradise," Jesus said to them. Yet he said, "There's rejoicing in the presence of angels." Who is it then in Glory Land that says, "Glory!" when somebody gets saved? It has to be God the Father. You may think He's not emotional, but Zephaniah 3:17 says that God will rejoice over you with singing. He will rejoice over you with singing. God sings, and I think God says, "Glory!" when somebody gets saved.

Why should God receive the glory? Because of His ability, His power to establish you. How? By the Gospel, the preaching of Jesus, the revelation of the mystery. Paul is writing to Gentiles, the Romans, and he says we're one in Christ.

But now is made manifest, and by the scriptures of the prophets, according to the commandment of the everlasting God, made known to all nations for the obedience of faith. — Romans 16:26

Just think about all that God is doing, all that God has done, all that God will do. He is to be receiving our glory, our praise, our exaltation, because of Who He is and what He has done.

Who is to Give Glory?

One of the ways glory is used is in reference to light. "And the glory of the Lord shone round about them: and they were sore afraid." (Luke 2:9) There was light, and the glory of the Lord came down. "Let your light so shine before men, that they may see your wood works, and glorify your Father which is in heaven." (Matthew 5:16) Jesus was preaching to Jews, by the way. We apply this to the church, but it is the Jewish nation who was to be a light for the Gentiles, according to Isaiah 42:6:

I the LORD have called thee in righteousness, and will hold thine hand, and will keep thee, and give thee for a covenant of the people, for a light of the Gentiles. — Isaiah 42:6

Jesus is called "the glory of My people Israel." (Luke 2:32) God even says, "Israel is My glory. I boast in them." (Isaiah 45:25) It's amazing! The meaning of this word "glory" just keeps growing. But in Matthew 5:16, who is to give glory?

Let your light so shine before men, that they may see your good works, and glorify your Father which is in heaven. — Matthew 5:16

Everybody! The whole universe is to give glory. Psalm 19:1 says, "The heavens declare the glory of God."

O sing unto the LORD a new song: sing unto the LORD, all the earth. Sing unto the LORD, bless his name; shew forth his salvation from day to day. Declare his glory among the heathen. — Psalm 96:1-3

How is Glory to be Given to Him?

Romans 16 is filled with examples of ways that people have given glory to God.

I commend unto you Phebe our sister, which is a servant of the church which is at Cenchrea [a seaport coast near

Corinth] that ye receive her in the Lord, as becometh saints, and that ye assist her in whatsoever business she hath need of you: for she hath been a succourer of many, and of myself also. — Romans 16:1-2

Phebe was a supporter, a helper. She was bringing glory to God by being a succourer, a helper to many. Do you want to glorify God? Be of service to somebody. The whole chapter is full of these examples.

Greet Priscilla and Aquila my helpers in Christ Jesus: Who have for my life laid down their own necks: unto whom not only I give thanks, but also all the churches of the Gentiles. — Romans 16:3-4

Priscilla and Aquila are an interesting couple. They're mentioned six times in the New Testament, and they're the ones who instructed Apollos more plainly in the way of the Gospel. According to 1 Corinthians 16, they had a church in their house. In 2 Timothy 4, they were serving with Timothy in Ephesus. These two people were on three different continents, and they served the Lord wherever they were. They worked with Paul as tent makers. These were marvelous people! These are people who, for Paul's life, have risked their own neck. That's beyond us in America.

Likewise greet the church that is in their house. Salute my wellbeloved Epaenetus, who is the firstfruits of Achaia unto Christ. — Romans 16:5

Epaenetus was Paul's first convert in southern Greece.
Greet Mary, who bestowed much labour on us. Salute Andronicus and Junia, my kinsmen, and my fellow prisoners, who are of note among the apostles, who also were in Christ before me. Greet Amplias my beloved in the Lord. Salute Urbane, our helper in Christ, and Stachys my beloved. Salute Apelles approved in Christ. — Romans 16:6-10

On and on and on it goes.

Salute Tryphena and Tryphosa, who labour in the Lord. Salute the beloved Persis, which laboured much in the Lord. Salute Rufus chosen in the Lord, and his mother and mine.
— Romans 16:12-13

Paul names these people. While they are just names to us, these were human, flesh-and-blood believers, your brothers and sisters in Christ. And how did they glorify God? They glorified God by being of service to other people. They were helpers. They labored. They risked their lives. They didn't sit back and wait to be ministered to. They followed Christ and ministered to Paul and to others. Some of them gave money. Some of them gave shelter. Some of them worked alongside Paul as tent makers. They served in various ways, but they all had a heart to serve. That's how you glorify God. You are not your own. Glorify God in your body and in your spirit, which are God's.

When is Christ to be Glorified?
Romans 16:26 said, "made known to all nations for the obedience of faith." That's an interesting phrase, because the first chapter of Romans says:

Paul, a servant of Jesus Christ, called to be an apostle, separated unto the gospel of God, (Which he had promised afore by his prophets in the holy scriptures,) Concerning his Son Jesus Christ our Lord, which was made of the seed of David according to the flesh; And declared to be the Son of God with power, according to the spirit of holiness, by the resurrection from the dead: By whom we have received grace and apostleship, for obedience to the faith.
— Romans 1:1-5

That's the what. "Among all nations"—that's the where. "For His name"—that's the why.

When is Christ to be glorified? Forever! Are you in Christ? Are you glorifying Christ? Are you obedient to the faith? "I've kept the faith" doesn't mean I've shielded it, protected it, and kept it to myself. No, keeping the faith involves the furthering of the faith. For if faith is kept by you and not shared with others, then faith dies when you die. You've got to obey the faith among all nations. For His name, AMEN!

Chapter Twelve

How to Rejoice Evermore
1 Thessalonians 5

How to Rejoice Evermore
1 Thessalonians 5

The first book of the New Testament to be written was I Thessalonians. This letter to the Church of Thessalonica predates Matthew, Mark, Luke, and John. It predates all other letters that Paul has written to the church. As he approaches the end of the book, he begins to give these short, pithy statements.

Rejoice evermore. — 1 Thessalonians 5:16

Is that "Pollyanna"? Is that too much idealism? Is that encouragement? Is that just a cliché? Or is that in fact an exhortation? It's an exhortation. The words are in the imperative. They are yelling from the page.

I would like to see a book written where emotions are expressed in color. Peaceful things could be a nice shade of blue. Angry things could be black. Some things could be purple or red. Cowardly things could be yellow. I'd like to see a book written three-dimensionally. If you're just doing simple declarative sentences, it would only be so high. But if you're asking a question, the words would tilt up. And if you were yelling, the letters would be a couple of inches tall. That would be a tough book to carry, but you'd get more out of it. You really would. But as it is, when you look at words, they are just black on white. They are flat. What the word in 1 Thessalonians 5:16 is saying is, *"Rejoice!"* The words are yelling.

The word *rejoice* means to bring joy again, joy the second time, joy still yet another time, and do that forever more. Rejoice continually. It is an exhortation. "Well," you might say, "those are just words." No, those are not just words. That's as much inspired as John 3:16. How is it then that you're going to be able to live up to 1 Thessalonians 5:16? Rejoice ever-more. How are you going to do that? Does it mean that you go around with a silly grin on your face all the time? I don't think that's what it means at all. Rather, it has the idea of letting joy come still yet another time.

I submit to you that the reason there are so many Christian people who look like they've been living with their face in a dill pickle barrel is that they have never learned what it is to let joy come still yet again. The truth is we live far beneath our privi-leges. There's a vast difference between the ground we occupy and the ground we could occupy. Rejoice again. Joy again. Let the joy come still yet another time, and still yet another time.

Now, how is it possible to do that? Let me suggest to you that, in the following verses, Paul gives the ways or the steps to incorporate joy into your life. These steps will help you to rejoice again, to joy still yet another time.

Pray Without Ceasing
Pray without ceasing. — 1 Thessalonians 5:17

Does that mean that you're never supposed to sleep? No, that's a human impossibility. What it does mean is that you are to have, without the omission of any occasion, prayer. Without ceasing means without missing any opportunity, without the omission of any occasion.

Three times the word unceasing or without ceasing is used in this first book of Thessalonians. Paul says, "I remember without ceasing" (1 Thess. 1:3). In chapter 2, he says, "We thank God without ceasing." Now, does that mean that he did nothing other than thank God for them? No, it doesn't mean that at all. It means that at every opportunity, at every occasion, without the omission of any opportunity, he gave thanks. And here it is the same idea, that you pray without missing any occasion to pray. You cannot let the joy come still yet another time unless you learn what it is to pray without the omission of any occa-sion.

You are never any greater than when you're in prayer. You

never realize your potential any greater than when you're praying. So why is it that we do everything other than pray? Two fellows were talking about their difficult circumstances. Things were so bad that one guy said, "Well, I guess we'll just have to pray." Then the other one responded, "Oh my, has it come to that?" Why is it that we find it easier to plan, find it easier to scheme, find it easier to organize, find it easier to advertise, find it easier to do everything than to pray?

One reason is that prayer requires total honesty. You can pull the wool over my eyes—and it be half plastic—and I'd believe it was wool. But you can't pull the wool over God's eyes. It's really a scary thing to pray. Suddenly you realize, "I'm in contact with the Creator of the universe. I better be careful what I say."

Pray without the omission of any occasion. You're not going to be able to let the joy come again unless you start at this point, for it is through prayer that you have contact with God. You're never going to approach the ideal of Verse 16 without first giving obedience to the admonition of Verse 17. I don't know anybody who rejoices evermore except when that person is strong in prayer. Maybe one reason we have so little joy is that we have so little prayer.

Give Thanks

A second admonition we must follow would be an attitude of thanksgiving.

In every thing give thanks: for this is the will of God in Christ Jesus concerning you. — 1 Thessalonains 5:18

I have a preacher friend by the name of Bill Davis whom I love to ask the same question, because he always gives the same answer. Whether it's in person, on the phone, on the platform, or wherever, I ask him, "How's Bill Davis?" I always ask him because I know what he's going to say. And he always says, "Better than I deserve." The fun part is it's nothing less than genuine with him. He means it. He is a thankful man, always with an attitude of thanksgiving. Do you have it?

You can never rejoice evermore, you can never be happy in the Lord, you can never have occasion for the joy to come again, unless you start with praying without ceasing, without the omission of any occasion. And that prayer is to be marked with thanksgiving.

Let me suggest to you that you should have a time of prayer in which you thank God for what He didn't do. I tell you, it'll bless you seven ways from Sunday. "Lord, I thank You that You didn't make me deaf. I thank You that You didn't make me blind. I thank You that You saved me when I was eleven instead of waiting until I was twenty-two. I thank You that You didn't let me be born in some corner of the world where I didn't know the Gospel. I thank You that You didn't let me be brain damaged. I thank You that You didn't put me in a wheelchair." Just start thanking God for what He has spared you from encountering. That'll bless your heart.

By then, you'll be so happy that you won't be able to hold yourself together to thank Him for what He has done. Rejoicing, an attitude of thanksgiving, and being thankful is essential to good mental health. It's doubly essential to have good spiritual health. Do you want the joy to come again? Thank God. Let your attitude be one of thanksgiving in everything.

Live in the Spirit's Control
Thirdly, allow the Holy Spirit to control. Now, that's simply stated, but it's awfully big.

Quench not the Spirit. — 1 Thessalonains 5:19

The Holy Spirit is to act as the governor upon your life. He is to act as the control on your life. You have only two spheres in which you can operate. You can either operate in the power of the flesh, or you can operate in the power of the Spirit.

To operate in the power of the flesh, you can depend on your experience or your education. Do you remember the first time you ever taught a Sunday School class? You shook all over. Did you stay up late the night before, praying? "God, oh God, oh God, maybe You can come before morning, huh?" Then He didn't come before morning. "Oh God, You've got to help me." Do you remember? Now it's the same old stuff, and it's easy to wait until Saturday night and look over the lesson, write down a few thoughts. The fear is gone, but the joy is gone, too.

The tendency is to depend upon your experience, to depend upon your learning, your education, to depend upon your personality, to depend upon yourself. When will we ever learn that Jesus knew what He was talking about in John 15, when He said, "Without Me, you can do nothing"? Paul gave the other side of that coin in Philippians 4:13: "I can do all things through Christ who strengtheneth me." The Holy Spirit is to control. He is to act as a governor upon your life. The idea of the filling of the Spirit is not quantity like half full or three-quarters full. It is rather an idea of control, of government, that I live under the control of the Holy Spirit, that He acts as that governing agency upon my life.

When things would go badly, my dad would say, "Now son, don't get puffed down." I asked him, "What's puffed down?" He said, "The opposite of puffed up." Sometimes he would say, "Now, don't get puffed up." I remember when I was in grade school and there was a play, I tried out and got the lead in the 5th grade play. I came home, "Guess who's going to be the star in the play?" My daddy asked, "Who?" And I told him, "I am." He said, "You may have the main role, but you may not be the star. Don't get puffed up." And through the years there was that constant "don't get puffed up" and "don't get puffed down."

I was in college, and we were traveling together one summer. He was preaching, and I was singing. As we were going down the road, I said, "Daddy, I think I finally learned what you meant in 'puffed up' and 'puffed down.'" He asked, "What's that?" I said, "You're saying let your moderation be known unto all men." He said, "That's exactly what I'm saying."

Don't get so high. Don't get so low. Don't get puffed up in yourself. Don't get puffed down in yourself. If you're under the control of the governing power of the Holy Spirit, there is no reason not to let the joy come again. You can't help it. It will come. Rejoice evermore. How? By allowing the Holy Spirit to control.

Do you know that you can be as poor or as good a Christian as you choose to be? Paul says in Romans 12, "I beseech you therefore, brethren, that you present your bodies a living sacrifice." "I can't command you. I beg you on the basis of the mercies of God, that you present your bodies a living sacrifice." You allow the Holy Spirit to control. That's a day by day, sometimes an hour by hour thing to allow the Spirit to control you.

Give Allegiance to the Word
Despise not prophesyings. — 1 Thessalonians 5:20

The idea is giving allegiance to the Word. The same word prophesyings is translated elsewhere as preaching. He's saying to despise not preaching. Give allegiance to the Word. Faith cometh by hearing, and hearing by the Word of God. At the time that 1 Thessalonians was being written, it was the first book of the New Testament. The Gospels do not come until twelve or fifteen years later. God was still speaking through prophets. God was still speaking through people. In our day, now that the Word of God is complete, He speaks through this Word. Paul is saying, "Give allegiance to this Word." It is by this word that you'll have cause to let the joy come again. Rejoice evermore. You are never ever going to be able to live in this world and to live with your head above the mess and to rejoice, unless you do hear and give allegiance to the Word of God.

Now, we are not only in a famine of the preaching of the Word, but I fear we are in a famine of the hearing of the Word. "Oh, I believe the Bible to be the Word of God," we say. But then we go weeks without ever reading it. It's amazing. We read everything else. If you only read things other than the Bible, I don't wonder why you have no joy. There are enough depressing stories in the newspaper. You need to give allegiance to the Word of God.

Prove All Things

But Paul didn't stop there. In Verse 21, he said:

Prove all things; hold fast that which is good.
— 1 Thessalonians 5:21

What he's saying is to ascertain the truth. Find out on your own. Dig it out. It bothers me when people say, "My preacher said so and so." Your preacher may not be right in what he says about such and such or so and so. You ought to be able to say, "My Bible says," and give it to yourself. I don't care who your preacher is. You cannot expect any one person to feed you enough spiritual strength and spiritual truth in a message or two a week. There is no one person who can give you enough to chew on that you're going to have a well-balanced diet for the rest of the week. You're going to have to do it on your own. That's "prove all things." Look into the book yourself. Find out for yourself. Prove all things. Ascertain the truth. Don't be carried away by every wind of doctrine. Know the Book. The more I know about the Word of God, the easier it is for me to rejoice evermore.

As a Biblical realist, I am not dependent upon what happens tomorrow in this world for my stability. The more you know the Book, the easier it is going to be for you to be happy in the Lord, to rejoice evermore.

Hate Evil

Then we come to a negative in Verse 22. If you would rejoice evermore:

Abstain from all appearance of evil. — 1 Thessalonians
5:22

He not only said to abstain from activity that is evil, but he said from all appearance of evil.

There are two things essential to being a good gardener, to being a good farmer. This is the first time in several years that we have not had a garden, my wife Fleta and I. We've got flower gardens this year that are gorgeous. Or rather, she has flower gardens this year. I dig up the ground and get it ready for her, and she does the rest of the work. But when we had a garden, two things were essential. The one I was good at is that you've got to love to eat the result. But the other is that you've got to hate weeds. It's no good to love the green beans unless you also hate weeds. Eventually, you won't be able to find the green beans in the midst of all the weeds. The weeds will choke out the growth of the green beans, and you're going to end up with just pods and no beans.

If you say, "I love the good!" then you've also got to hate evil. The truth is most of us are, at best, just kind of neutral about evil. Do you hate evil? You can't just say, "I love the Lord." You've also got to hate sin. And you really can't love the Lord unless you hate sin. The idea of abstaining from every appearance of evil is not only good Bible teaching, but this is all good mental health. Why is it important? The Bible says in James 1:8 that a double minded man is unstable in all his ways. If you fill your mind with good and evil, you are becoming a spiritual schizophrenic, double minded. The problem with most of us is not that we don't love the Lord. The problem with most of us is we just don't hate sin. Abstain from all appearance of evil.

Be Sanctified

The result of all of that is Verse 23, the first part of it.

And the very God of peace sanctify you wholly.
— 1 Thessalonians 5:23

Spirit, soul, and body sanctified. Don't be afraid of the word sanctified. It's a good word. The Old Testament speaks of things being sanctified. The instruments, the furniture in the tabernacle, a table of showbread, a lamp stand, a brazen altar, a laver—things were sanctified. The Bible speaks of a place being sanctified: "The place whereon thou standest, Moses, that place is sanctified ground, holy ground" (Exodus 3:5). The temple was another place that was sanctified. The Bible also speaks of people being sanctified: "Separate now unto Me Aaron and the sons of Aaron. I will sanctify them unto Myself to do the work of the priesthood" (Exodus 30:30). So you have places and things and people all spoken of as being sanctified. That's a good Bible word. Don't be afraid of it.

However, being sanctified is not a second work of grace. That would be to say there was something weak and ineffective with the first work. And the first work is the only work. Instead, sanctification is a divine process that starts the moment you are saved and continues until the moment you go home to be with the Lord. By circumstances, by the indwelling presence of the Holy Spirit, by the Word of God, by the instruction in the Word —anything and everything that happens to you—God designed to conform you to the image of His own Son. Being sanctified means that you are set apart from. It means, secondly, that you are set apart to.

For example, the sons of Aaron were to separate from the other people of Israel to God. Separate them FROM. Separate them TO Me. Separate them FOR. That's sanctification—to separate from, to separate to, to separate for. We are sanctified from the world, to the Lord, for the purpose of serving.

Paul says very practical things. If you will do these things, you will not only be able to let the joy come again, and again, and again, and rejoice evermore, but you will be totally sanctified from, to, and for. It doesn't have a thing to do with sinless perfection. It has an idea of setting apart from, setting apart to, and setting apart for. From the world, to the Lord, for service. How is your sanctification? How is your rejoicing? Amen? AMEN!